THE HISTORY OF ISRAEL

THE HISTORY OF ISRAEL
ITS FACTS AND FACTORS

by

H. WHEELER ROBINSON, M.A., D.D.

*Late Principal of Regent's Park College and Reader
in Biblical Criticism in the University of Oxford*

SECOND EDITION, REVISED BY

L. H. BROCKINGTON M.A., B.D.

*Senior Lecturer in Aramaic and Syriac in
the University of Oxford*

GERALD DUCKWORTH & CO. LTD.
3 Henrietta Street, London, W.C.2

First published 1938
Reprinted 1940, 1941, 1947
1952, 1954, 1957, 1960

Second edition 1964

© 1964 by GERALD DUCKWORTH & CO LTD

*Printed in Great Britain by Richard Clay and Company, Ltd.,
Bungay, Suffolk*

PREFACE

THE purpose of this short history of Israel is to meet the need felt by many teachers and students for an introductory text-book covering the whole ground, and suitable as a preparation for the use of the larger histories, and of studies of special periods. The title indicates the nature of the book. I have tried to include all the chief *facts* which emerge from the literary and epigraphic sources, whilst showing throughout the shaping *factors* of the history, particularly its succession of imperial backgrounds. The book is intended to be complementary to my previous one in this series, viz., *The Religious Ideas of the Old Testament*. I have therefore in this book refrained from any detailed discussion of the religion, though it is impossible to write a true history of Israel which does not always keep religion in sight, either as cause or effect— as cause, in the creation and maintenance of the nation, and as effect, in the deposit of 'Scriptures' which became fundamental to both Judaism and Christianity, and also (indirectly) to Islam. Whilst my treatment of the history is 'realistic', assuming as it does the constant operation of those psychical, political and economic forces which work amongst all peoples, it is not intended to be 'naturalistic'. I have therefore felt that it was germane to my purpose to include a final chapter[1] on the philosophy of history as illustrated by the history of Israel. This chapter makes explicit the assumptions on which the facts and factors of the history of Israel have been handled in this book. As a distinguished Old Testament

[1] Originally given as presidential address to the Oxford Society for Historical Theology.

scholar[1] has said, 'The historian of particular historical developments cannot pursue his researches or set forth his results without the aid of the general concepts and ideas provided for him by the philosophy of history.' It is consequently better to make explicit what would otherwise be implicit, and there is a special reason for this in regard to the Old Testament. The only adequate basis for a philosophy of Christian revelation is a philosophy of the history which created the Old Testament, and crowned that splendid literature with the New.

I am grateful to the Rev. A. J. D. Farrer, who read the typescript, and to the Rev. Professor H. H. Rowley, who read the proof, for many useful criticisms; also to the Rev. L. H. Brockington, who has compiled the Index.

H. WHEELER ROBINSON.

Oxford,
        Easter, 1938.

[1] W. Eichrodt, 'Hat die alttestamentliche Theologie noch selbst ändige Bedeutung innerhalb der alttestamentlichen Wissenschaft?' in *Zeitschrift für die alttestamentliche Wissenschaft,* 1929, p. 86.

PREFACE TO SECOND EDITION

THE need for a new edition of this book to meet the continuing demand has given opportunity for some slight revision. It has to be recognized that a history of Israel is at the same time an interpretation of the meaning of that history. It was always Wheeler Robinson's aim to interpret the Old Testament and the history of the people of Israel in the light of God's plan of redemption. Any major revision may well have interfered with the author's pattern of interpretation. For this reason attention has been given mainly to revision of dates, spelling of names and other incidental matters.

L. H. BROCKINGTON.

Oxford, 1963

CONTENTS

vii

CONTENTS

I.—THE LAND AND THE PEOPLE

ALL history is an ellipse, of which the land and the people are the two foci. Each is itself a complex group of factors. The physical factors which spring from the land are due to its position in relation to the lands of other peoples, from which will issue commercial relations and military fortunes; to the nature of the land itself, which will decide its economic conditions and inner divisions; to the climate, which will affect both the character and the prosperity of the people. The spiritual factors which spring from the people are chiefly to be seen in its political and religious developments—the kind of state which it creates for itself to protect its social life, and the attitude towards the world of things unseen which finds expression in religious beliefs and customs. The two groups of factors are constantly passing into one another, as do body and soul in the individual life; the economic conditions, for instance, will shape the national character and be themselves modified by it. If we could write history as God sees it, the two foci of our ellipse would coalesce into the centre of a circle. This remark has a particular bearing on our subject. The importance of the history of Israel consists in its religion, which profoundly affected the national fortunes at critical periods; without the religion, the history would be inexplicable and ultimately insignificant.

History might be called the sacrament of the religion of Israel; through the history of Israel, she saw the face of God and endured as seeing Him who is invisible. But the details of that history with which we shall be concerned—the words and deeds, the thoughts and emotions, and above all the persistent purposes of the Israelites—these were the bread and

1

wine of the sacrament, which the touch of God transformed
into both the symbol and the instrument of His grace for all
time. We cannot properly understand the religion without
knowing the history, and knowing it, so far as is now possible
to us, in its original and actual form. If it is what it so often
claims to be—the history of God's mighty acts (Ps. 106:2),
as well as of man's responses to them—then the history will
ultimately reveal the purposes of God through the issues of
the purposes of men. The test of the process will be in its
results, rather than in any particular details of it. 'If thou
take forth the precious from the common, thou shalt be as
my mouth.' That word to the prophet Jeremiah (15:19)
might well express the true process of inspiration and
revelation.

1. THE LAND

The land of Israel, i.e., Palestine, is the southern half
(more exactly, two-fifths) of Syria, which is the fertile north-
west coast-land of Arabia. Thus Palestine forms, with the
river-lands of the Tigris and the Euphrates, the western half
of what has been fitly called the 'fertile' crescent. Syria is
roughly 400 miles long and from 70 to 100 miles broad, with
the Lebanon mountains dividing Palestine in the south from
the rest of Syria in the north. From the heights of Lebanon
flow four rivers—the Orontes north to Antioch, the Abana
east to Damascus, the Litany west to the Mediterranean, and
the Jordan south to the Dead Sea. The great gorge of the
Jordan, continued south of the Dead Sea by the valley of the
Arabah, divides a continuous range of hills on the east from
the more broken range on the west. The western range is
broken particularly by the valley of Jezreel, opening into the
plain of Esdraelon—just as if the range at this point had been
swung bodily westwards away from the hills of Galilee to
form the projection of Carmel. Apart from this great break,
we may think of Palestine as consisting of four lines of
country running parallel with each other from north to south,
viz., the maritime plain, the western plateau, the Jordan

valley and the eastern plateau. The first result of all this
variety of configuration is that the inhabitants will tend to
live in regional groups of different character. It has been well
said that Palestine is 'emphatically a land of tribes'.[1] In
regard to the position of the land, on the thoroughfare of the
'fertile crescent', we see at once the not less inevitable inter-
relation of Palestine with the two great centres of early
civilization lying to east and west—Babylonia and Egypt.
Military invasion and commercial travel do not move as the
crow flies; they follow the practicable lines of communication. This means that Palestine, especially its coast-road,
was the direct link between the east and the west. We shall
see the effects of this position all through the history of
Israel, beginning with the Babylonian–Egyptian culture of
those whom Israel found in possession of the land, and ending
with the imperial necessities which led to the banishment
of the Jews from Palestine by the Romans. The central
position meant that the land became the focus of all kinds
of cultural influences and ideas, Babylonian and Assyrian,
Egyptian, Persian, Greek and Roman, as one great empire
after another dominated the stage. Moreover—and this was
a matter of the greatest importance to Israel, and constantly
influenced its history—Palestine was always easily accessible
to waves of nomadic immigration from the desert. It was
bordered by a half-circle of semi-nomadic peoples always
liable to be forced into the more settled land through the
pressure of nomads upon them, or through sheer economic
necessity. The western boundary was more definite; not only
was there the Mediterranean, but the coastal land was
occupied by the Philistines in the south and by the Phoenicians in the north; Israel hardly ever gained a foothold on the
coast. If we consider the western range of hill-country, we see
Galilee in the north, always more or less detached from the
rest of the land, with the great plain lying to the south of it.
This northern part was well-watered and very fertile. The

[1] Sir George Adam Smith, *The Historical Geography of the Holy Land*,
p. 59 (ed. 4).

plain of Esdraelon (Megiddo) played a great part in the
military history of the land, because it afforded the natural
way to and from Damascus and the East; it had a number of
fortified towns, viz., Megiddo, Taanach, Ibleam, Jezreel and
Beth-shean. The hill-country of Ephraim and of Judah south
of the plain is less varied than that of Galilee; the important
towns from Shechem to Hebron in the extreme south are
naturally on the watershed. In the north there were grown
corn, vines and olives; in the south the country was mainly
pastoral.[1] Across the Jordan, there was the northern plain,
including Bashan, fertile in wheat, which the Aramaeans
were to make their own. South of the Yarmuk there was
Gilead, also fertile, which extended as far as the Jabbok.
North and south of the Arnon the country was occupied by
Ammon and Moab. Edom lay south of the Dead Sea.

As for climate, there were the two strongly contrasted
seasons of summer and winter, and the equally contrasted
west winds from the sea and east winds from the desert.
In the rainy season from November to April, there was the
early autumn rain (*moreh*), before the ploughing, the heavy
winter rain (*geshem*), and the spring rain (*malqosh*); after this,
the vegetation had to depend upon the abundant dew. On
the whole the country was agricultural, its chief products
being corn, wine and olive-oil.[2] Settlement in Canaan would
mean the adoption of a new culture by nomads, deeply
affecting both social and religious life, since these are always
closely linked amongst ancient peoples. It has even been
said of these two different kinds of life, the nomadic and the
agricultural, that 'The key to the history of pre-exilic Israel,
both in religion and in secular affairs, is to be found in the
reaction of these two points of view upon one another.'[3]

Archaeology has shown that Palestine had its Stone Age,

[1] The 'wilderness' (*midhbar*) of Judaea (Jos 15:61, 62) denotes its
'pasturage'; the word *midhbar* really means 'a driving-ground for cattle'.
Cf. Joel 2:22, Ps. 65:13.

[2] K. Galling (*Die Israelitische Staatsverfassung*, p. 50) points out that
the three fruit-trees of Jotham's fable are the olive, the fig and the vine.

[3] T. H. Robinson, *The History of Israel*, Preface, p. x.

and was inhabited long before the dawn of history.[1] From about 3000 B.C. to the fall of Babylon about 1600 B.C., Syria was controlled by the kings of lower Mesopotamia; after that, Egypt secured more influence over Palestine, particularly when the Semitic invaders of Egypt known as the Hyksos were driven from Egypt (about 1580). The Egyptian power over Syria was established by Thutmosis (Thothmes) III, at the important battle of Megiddo in 1483. Half a century or so after this we enter what is known as the Tell el-Amarna Age, in which the state of affairs in Palestine fortunately becomes clearer to us. But as this is the period at which some of the Hebrews may have begun to enter Palestine, it is necessary first to state what is known of the racial origins of Israel.

2. THE PEOPLE

According to the genealogical scheme found in Gen. 10, 11, Israel traced its origin through 'Eber' (the Hebrews) back to Shem, the eldest of those three sons of Noah who are represented as the source of all mankind. For this reason, modern scholars call the group of nations which spoke or speak languages more or less closely allied to Hebrew the Semites (using the Greek form 'Sem' instead of the Hebrew 'Shem'), though the actual classification given in Genesis is not ethnologically correct or complete. According to the patriarchal traditions which are attached to this scheme, the history of the chosen people began with the migration of Abram from Babylonia up the Euphrates to Harran (Gen. 11:31). Another reference (Josh 24:2, 3) says that up to this point the ancestors of Israel 'served other gods', and that it was at this point that God chose Abraham (Abram) and brought him into Canaan. He was accompanied by his nephew Lot, from whom Moab and Ammon, related to Israel but disliked by them, are said to have been derived after a dishonourable fashion (Gen. 19:30–38).

[1] It has been shown that the occupation of the site of Jericho can be traced back to at least 6800 B.C. A popular account of the excavations at Jericho can be found in Kathleen Kenyon, *Digging up Jericho*, 1957.

According to Hebrew tradition, therefore, the ancestor of Israel was linked with three important centres of Semitic life, viz. Babylonia, Harran and Canaan.[1] Harran is apparently 'the city of Nahor', Abraham's brother, to whom his steward was sent to find a wife for Isaac (Gen. 24:10); it is located in Aram-naharaim. The three districts serve to remind us of the three principal Semitic migrations, possibly from Arabia, which laid the foundation for the subsequent history of nearer Asia:

(1) The Accadian or Babylonian–Assyrian into Mesopotamia, possibly as early as 3000 B.C.

(2) The 'Canaanite', including Phoenicians, Moabites, Ammonites, Edomites, say between 2000 and 1600 B.C.

(3) The Aramaean, centring in Damascus, but largely represented by nomad Semites—'wandering Aramaeans' like Jacob (Deut. 26:5, R.V. *mar.*)—who come into prominence about 1350 B.C.

It is with this third group, the Aramaeans, that the Hebrew traditions especially linked Abraham; this is confirmed by the story of the relations of Jacob and Laban. The Hebrew *language*, however, as distinct from racial origins, belongs to the Canaanite section of the north-western group (Aramaic, Phoenician, Moabite, etc.), the other groups being the eastern (Babylonian), and the south-western (Arabic). Hebrew is 'the language of Canaan' (Is. 19:18).

3. PALESTINE IN THE AMARNA AGE (c. 1400)

In 1887 there were discovered at Tell el-Amarna, midway between Cairo and Thebes (the residence of the kings Amenophis III and IV), about 360 tablets of official correspondence between these kings and those of Babylon, Assyria, the Mitanni and Hittites, together with the vassal-chieftains

---

[1] It is sometimes held that there was another 'Ur' in upper Mesopotamia, and that originally Abraham was represented as coming from it, rather than from 'Ur of the Chaldees'; see Lods, *Israel*, E. T., pp. 165, 6, and cf. Skinner on Gen. 11:31, 32.

of Egypt in Palestine. The letters[1] are mostly those written *to* Pharaoh. They imply the imperial position of Egypt to which the victories of Thutmosis III had raised her, but they also show that this position was about to be lost, both within and without Palestine. When Amenophis III died (*c.* 1370), the crucial moment had come; only an energetic and militant ruler could have saved the Egyptian Empire. Instead of this, the Pharaoh who succeeded him (Ikhnaton) was a religious revolutionary, who bitterly alienated his own powerful priesthood and utterly neglected his now declining rule over the subject states. This explains the anarchy into which Palestine fell, the anarchy which is so constantly illustrated in these letters, appealing as they do for help against invaders or plotters and sometimes offering flattering excuses for the plotting itself. There was much civil war amongst the chieftains, each eager for self-aggrandisement. The invaders now seizing their opportunity in a time of Egypt's weakness were chiefly the Hittites and the Ḥabiru.

The Hittites, who at this time[2] obtained supremacy over northern Syria and north-western Mesopotamia, and kept it for a couple of centuries, were a non-Semitic people of Cappadocia. At their capital, Boghaz-keui, some of their records in Babylonian (cuneiform) and in half a dozen Indo-European dialects were discovered in 1907. Surviving monuments show the great extent of their empire in the thirteenth century—Asia Minor, most of Syria and upper Mesopotamia. As a people they can be traced back as far as *c.* 1600 B.C., when they raided Babylonia. Rameses II of Egypt checked them at the battle of Kadesh (in the Orontes valley), and made a treaty with them in 1278, by which Palestine was left to Egypt. About 1200 the Hittites seem to have been

---

[1] A selection of the most important will be found in J. B. Pritchard, *Ancient Near Eastern Texts relating to the Old Testament*, 2nd Ed. 1955 [*A.N.E.T.*] pp. 483 ff.

[2] In the Amarna letters, they appear as threatening Rib-addi of Byblus and Abimilki of Tyre. The governor of the Amurru in the Lebanon and Anti-Lebanon districts eventually found it expedient to pass over to the Hittites.

B

overpowered by hordes from the north, which also pressed on into Egypt. In 1100 they were still holding Carchemish and the surrounding districts. In the latter part of the eighth century they were absorbed into the Assyrian Empire. The Hittites who are so often named in the Old Testament as living in Palestine seem to have been offshoots of this once imperial people. In Gen. 10:15, their eponymous ancestor is 'Heth', the son of 'Canaan'. Abraham is represented as buying the cave of Machpelah from a Hittite settlement at Hebron (Gen. 23).

The Ḥabiru were Semitic Bedouin of the Aramaean branch. They appear in many parts of Palestine at this time, e.g., against Rib-Addi of Byblus[1] and Abdi-Ḥiba of Jerusalem; the latter, in fact, seems to be surrounded by enemies. Etymologically, the name Ḥabiru can be identified with that of the 'Hebrews', though we must not hastily assume that these 'Hebrews' were the Israelites with whom is our own concern. The Ḥabiru may have been distant kinsmen and forerunners of the Israelites, who settled in Canaan and gradually merged into the general mass of Canaanites, and were ultimately absorbed by the Israelites. It is quite possible that the 'Israel' in Canaan conquered by Merneptah of Egypt about 1230 was a branch of the Ḥabiru, not denoting the Israelites of the Biblical Exodus at all (see Ch. II).

4. THE PATRIARCHAL AGE AND NOMADISM

In the strict sense, a history of Israel begins only with the exodus from Egypt and the settlement in Canaan, because prior to this there was no nation to be called 'Israel'. But the Book of Genesis offers us two groups of narratives which take us back beyond these historic events to the very beginnings of the world. The first, consisting of the first eleven chapters of Genesis, is not 'history' in any sense of the word. It is 'myth', the embodiment in the form of narrative of popular

---

[1] Here they are called SA-GAZ, who are to be identified with the Ḥabiru; Gressmann, *ATAT*[2], p. 373.

ideas concerning the phenomena of nature and history. The myths of these early chapters have many points of contact with those of Babylonia, from which they were chiefly derived, though probably through Canaanite mediation. In the form of these myths, which account for some of the salient features of man's experience, such as the pains of child-bearing or the variety of human language, there is little that is distinctive of Israel; the distinctive feature is the moral and religious use to which these myths are put, the atmosphere in which they are told, in a word, the sense of God which they are made to exhibit. In this deep way, the unconscious product of the oral telling and retelling of the myth, it became more fitted to be the vehicle of a divine revelation than if it were history—more fitted not only because the very concept of history was absent in the times to which these myths go back, but also because their subject-matter, e.g., the creation of the world and the origin of moral evil, lies beyond human observation.

From the twelfth chapter of Genesis to the end of the book, we have the patriarchal stories,[1] to be distinguished from the earlier chapters as having some actual nucleus in history, whatever embellishments or amplifications the original events may have received. At first sight they seem to be the stories of individual lives, in all their wealth of graphic detail. More careful study, however, will show that they deal largely with the traditions of tribal movements and relations, rather than form the biographies of actual persons. The patriarchal legends, as we may properly call them, in distinction from the myths of the early chapters, are of real historical value, though it is not the value of a direct historical record. These stories of the patriarchs are undoubtedly true to life; they give us something of the immemorial life of the nomad or semi-nomad, still largely the same as it was then. They also, like the myths, enshrine the moral and religious ideas of the age in which they received their present form, say, from

---

[1] On these and their illustration of Israel's nomadic life, see E. Dhorme, *La Religion des Hébreux nomades* (1937).

the ninth century onwards[1]; the product, from the standpoint of literature, is of fascinating beauty and lasting
importance. But we cannot treat them as historical documents for the times of Hammurabi (c. 1750 B.C.) with whom
Abraham is perhaps represented as contemporary (Amraphel
in Gen. 14:1). There may quite well have been originals for
these typical portraits, but even if it could be proved by the
unexpected discovery of documentary evidence belonging to
the patriarchal period that Abraham, Isaac and Jacob were
the actual ancestors of Israel, the discovery would not greatly
add to our historical knowledge.[2] At this period prior to the
existence of the nation, the chief point of interest for us does
not lie in such individual happenings, but in racial affinities
and tribal movements. Such information can to some extent
be gathered already from these stories, which are indeed the
ancient and Oriental way of giving it, though with full belief
in the historicity of the patriarchs. We have already seen
how the story of Abraham's earlier movements illustrates or
rather describes one of the waves of Semitic migration into
Canaan. The story of Lot and his daughters' incest expresses
at once the sense of kinship with the Moabites and Ammonites, and Israel's dislike of, and hostility towards, these
peoples. So the stories go on to explain the Bedouin of the
desert from their ancestor Ishmael, and the Edomites of the
south country from Esau. The supremacy of Joseph in
Egypt reflects the subsequent supremacy of the Joseph-clans
(the northern kingdom in the later history); the twelve sons
of Jacob are a genealogical explanation of what were ulti-

---

[1] Cf. *The Old Testament, its Making and Meaning*, by H. Wheeler
Robinson, Ch. III, 3 (b).

[2] The identification of Terah, the father of Abraham (Gen. 11:24),
with the Terah of the Ras Shamra Tablets (Virolleaud, *La Légende de
Keret*, p. 25) is interesting chiefly for the growth of legend; Terah is
apparently a lunar deity as well as a tribal hero. Documents discovered
during excavations at Nuzu (northern Mesopotamia) and Mari (middle
Euphrates) have served to throw light on some social conditions and
legal practices of the patriarchal period. The documents are written in
Cuneiform script and in the Hurrian language (Biblical Horite) and
reflect a society in many ways resembling that of the Hebrew Patriarchs.

mately regarded as the twelve tribes of Israel, though their historical counterparts emerged gradually, and in a variety of ways. Something of this variety is already reflected in the distinction of the Leah and Rachel tribes from the 'concubine' tribes traced to Bilhah and Zilpah, in which there may have been a greater admixture of 'Canaanite' blood. How easily the narrative passes from the apparently individual to the tribal idea may be seen at many points. Thus, in Gen. 10:15, we read that Canaan, here represented as a grandson of Noah, 'begat Zidon his firstborn and Heth', where Zidon is a city and Heth a people (the Hittites). In Gen. 25, Keturah is introduced as a wife of Abraham, yet her sons and grandsons are obviously peoples, e.g., Midian. Recent excavations in Samaria have supplied a good example of this tendency to transform geography into history. The fragments of inscribed pottery (used as account-books) found in the palace of Ahab give about a score of *place-names* in the northern kingdom; six of them (Abi'ezer, Helek, Shechem, Shemida', No'ah and Hoglah) were already known to us from Josh 17:2, 3 (cf. Num. 26:30–33), but as the alleged *personal founders* of tribal divisions in Manasseh. The constructor of the genealogy doubtless worked on what seemed to him a perfectly legitimate principle, viz., that places found within a particular tribal district must have had a personal founder, who would be a descendant of the ancestor of the whole tribe. 'As the first four (of the names given above from the ostraka) have a masculine termination, and the remaining two have a feminine one, he has included the former among the male descendants and the latter among the female.'[1] If it be argued that the places *may* have had a personal founder, who *may* have been a descendant of Jacob, the answer is easy; Shechem, here given as a person, was a place so far back as the Tell el-Amarna letters, and probably earlier, so that it existed at a time when the Israelites had not yet entered Palestine.

It is clear from the patriarchal stories, as well as from

[1] Jack, *Samaria in Ahab's time*, p. 69.

much other evidence, that Israel conceived its ancestors to have been nomads; the description of Jacob in Deut. 26:5 (R.V. *mar.*) is of a 'wandering Aramaean'. The language itself preserves memories of this nomadic period; thus the verb which means to 'set out' (*nasa‘*) originally meant to 'pull up' tent-pegs (cf. Is. 33:20), whilst the word for 'pasturage' (*naweh*) can also mean 'dwelling'. This nomadic period, of course, is not to be confined to the generation *after* the Exodus; the return of 'Israel in Egypt' to the desert is simply a return to its former mode of life. The settlement in Canaan, however, meant the transition to the life of an agricultural people, tied to particular spots by the growing of corn and fruit-trees. The nomad, on the contrary, is restricted in his wanderings chiefly by the water-supply, on which depends the life of himself, his camels and sheep and goats. His social organization will be simple, except for its far-reaching kinships; it is that of the family grouped with other families into larger or smaller units to form the clan (*mish-pachah*), for the purposes of mutual protection, yet not in such large bodies as to exceed the water-supply of the area of its migrations. There is no official head to such a clan, other than the group of sheikhs exercising an authority chiefly moral, or the personal influence of an outstanding fighter. The primary sanction is naturally blood-revenge. If the individual is separated from his group, he finds it necessary, just as Charles Doughty did, to become the 'client' (Hebrew *ger*, the resident alien) of one of the groups. Doughty's *Arabia Deserta* has given us the classical picture of nomad life, drawn from our own times. The life of Israel's nomad ancestors must have been largely the same as that which Doughty so faithfully depicts. His pages help us to live amongst those far-off groups of men and women who finally drifted from their pasture-grounds in the south of Canaan to the borders of Egypt. There began the great experience which they and their descendants never forgot—the experience which welded them into a nation.

According to the well-known Biblical narrative, the migration of Jacob and his sons to the land of Goshen (Gen. 46:28) was undertaken at the invitation of Joseph, who after a series of surprising adventures had obtained a commanding position in the land of Egypt. Behind these dramatic and very moving stories, composed in a much later age, we can see the familiar spectacle of nomads settling on the borders of cultivated land, with Egyptian approval and in the position of a subject people. How long this period lasted we have no means of knowing. The definite statement of the Hebrew text[1] of Ex. 12:40, 41, that it was for 430 years is certainly inconsistent with that of Ex. 6:16ff. that Moses stood in the fourth generation from Levi. Whatever the length of the period of this semi-nomadic condition, it seems to have been terminated by the enforced labour extracted from them by a subsequent Pharaoh, followed by their revolt and escape, events with which the Book of Exodus opens.

[1] The Septuagint and the Samaritan versions, by adding 'and in the land of Canaan', reduce the period to 215 years, since half the whole period is supposed to lie between Abraham's entrance into Canaan and Jacob's into Egypt (Gen. 12:4; 21:5; 25:26; 47:9).

II.—THE EXODUS AND THE SETTLEMENT

1. EGYPT

THE first of the succession of great empires with which Israel was brought into contact was Egypt. Lower Egypt consists of the fan-shaped Delta of the Nile, with the modern Cairo at its apex, lying about 100 miles from the sea-front, which extends for 155 miles. This land has been deposited by the Nile itself, of which the deep valley, ten to fifteen miles wide for hundreds of miles south, then narrowing south of Thebes through the 'Cataracts' at Aswan as far as Wady Halfa, forms what is known as Upper Egypt. (The distance by river from Wady Halfa to the Mediterranean is given as 960 miles.) Thebes, at the semi-circular bend of the Nile, and more or less accessible from the Red Sea and the East, was the earliest centre of the civilization of the Nile.

The geographical division between Lower and Upper Egypt naturally led to a political one. This is reflected in the fact that when there arose a united kingdom of Egypt, its king was called 'lord of the two lands'. The history of ancient Egypt is divided into three 'kingdoms', known as the Old, the Middle and the New, each containing numerous dynasties. The Old Kingdom is dated from about 2778 to 2263 B.C. From its king Khufu (Cheops) comes the Great Pyramid of about 2500 B.C. The Old Kingdom came to an end in a period of general anarchy, out of which arose a Theban dynasty to found the Middle Kingdom (2263–1580). The most notable feature of it was the invasion of Egypt by the Hyksos or 'Shepherd-Kings', who specially concern us, because some scholars would connect them with 'Israel in Egypt'.

From about 2000 B.C. there had been pressure from

14

northern invaders (Aryans) upon both Mesopotamia and northern Syria. This led to a displacement of (Syrian) Semites towards Egypt, the result of which is seen in the Hyksos invasion of Egypt. The Hyksos were Semites. Their name is said to correspond with the Egyptian *Hiku-khasut*, 'princes of the foreign countries' ('Shepherd-kings' is due to Manetho's confusion with *shasu* 'Bedouin'). For a short time, the most powerful Hyksos king, viz., Khian, controlled Upper, as well as Lower, Egypt. Some of these kings seem to have Semitic names, viz., Ja'cob-el, 'Anath-el.[1] (There is also a possible Semitic link in the place-name, Tell el-Yehudiyeh, 'the mound of the Jewess'.) The Hyksos reigned for more than a century, from before 1700 to *c*. 1580, when they were expelled by the Theban kings of the south. Avaris, the Hyksos capital, was captured about 1578. The Hyksos were pursued into the Negeb (the country south of what later became Judaea), and were besieged in Sharuhen for three years. This foreign invasion and dominion is not only one of the important events in the history of Egypt, but is also of considerable interest to the student of Biblical history, because it has been linked with Israel's settlement there. This view was maintained by the Egyptian writer Manetho, *c*. 250 B.C., who is quoted with full approval by Josephus[2]— 'these shepherds were no other than our fathers'—as well as by some modern scholars,[3] though it is not easy to fit the Biblical story into such a framework.

The Hyksos were expelled by Ahmosis, the founder of the XVIIIth dynasty, with whom begins the New Kingdom or Period of the Empire. This is the period of the rise and fall of a foreign Egyptian Empire. In return for the Semitic invasion of Egypt, the Egyptians pressed into Semitic Syria and to the Euphrates, at a time when the Kassite power in Babylon was weak, and Assyria had not yet emerged. In

---

[1] Burney, *Judges*, p. lxvi.   [2] *Contra Apionem*, i, 14.

[3] e.g. H. R. Hall: 'the Exodus is the Expulsion of the Hyksos looked at from the peculiar angle of Jewish tradition' (*The People and the Book*, ed. Peake, p. 10); more fully in his book, *The Ancient History of the Near East* (ed. 8), pp. 403 ff.

these campaigns, the names of Thutmosis I (c. 1530) and especially Thutmosis III (1483–1450; the battle of Megiddo, 1483) are prominent, whilst Queen Hatshepsut, who came between them, and has been called 'the first great woman in history',[1] carried out great building enterprises at home. Under Amenophis III, who reigned till 1370, the Egyptian imperial power began to decline; under his successor, Amenophis IV (Ikhnaton), the religious reformer, the control of foreign affairs was lost. A revolt of the priests of the Theban Sun-god Ra brought the 'New Kingdom' to an end (1354). To the reigns of these last two kings belong the Tell el-Amarna letters, to which reference has already been made.

The next important ruler of Egypt was Rameses II, who came to the throne c. 1301. He conducted a series of vigorous campaigns in Syria against the Hittites, and won, though barely, the battle of Kadesh (Orontes valley). At home he was a great builder, and is known to have built (or rebuilt) the cities of Pithom and Raamses, east of the Delta. According to Ex. 1:11, these were built for him by Israelite labour, though there is no confirmation of this from contemporary Egyptian records. If we accept it, the Pharaoh of the oppression is definitely identified with Rameses II, who was still reigning about 1250. The Biblical narrative goes on to say that the Exodus took place under his successor (cf. Ex. 2:23, 24), whom we know to have been Merneptah, though again there is no confirming reference in the Egyptian annals. They do, however, refer to a number of victories won by Merneptah in Palestine (c. 1229), including the statement that 'Ysiraal is desolated, its seed is not.'[2] The significance of this must be considered in relation to the whole problem of the date of the Exodus.

---

[1] *The Cambridge Ancient History* (Vol. II, p. 61), which I have chiefly followed in the above statements.

[2] Given in Driver's *Exodus*, p. xxxix.

2. The Date of the Exodus

As to the date of the Exodus, and that of the subsequent settlement in Canaan, there is at present wide diversity of judgment amongst scholars,[1] and the present state of the evidence leaves no room for dogmatism. No adequate discussion of this can be given here, further than a statement of the chief grounds which incline the present writer to regard the Biblical tradition as valid, viz., that the Pharaoh of the oppression was Rameses II, and the Pharaoh of the Exodus his successor, Merneptah. The direct evidence for this (Ex. 1:11) ought not to be set aside as an interpolation; nor dismissed as mistaken, unless plainly irreconcilable with other valid evidence. It is true that archaeological evidence suggests that earlier cities existed on the probable site of Raamses.[2] We also know that the *Apiru*, whose name has been identified by some scholars with that of the Hebrews, were in Egypt both before and after the time of Rameses II, as well as being employed by him as workmen.[3] But in regard to the Apiru, as well as to the Ḥabiru of the Tell el-Amarna letters, such identification must not be pressed to the point of a definite identification of the whole groups concerned. We are not dealing with sharply defined unities, in the case of Apiru, Ḥabiru or Hebrews, or even of the Israelites themselves at this period. Kinsfolk of the Israelites may well have been the invaders of, and settlers in, Canaan in the fourteenth century, and other kinsfolk of theirs may have remained in Egyptian lands after the Israelite Exodus. Other evidence alleged for a 'Moses–Joshua' settlement in Canaan prior to the latter half of the thirteenth century is not conclusive. The most important is the Merneptah stele[4] of 1229. All that this can be taken to prove is that at that date

[1] See J. W. Jack, *The Date of the Exodus* (1925), who argues for 1445 B.C., and T. H. Robinson, *History of Israel* (1932), who favours 'the early part of the fifteenth century' (p. 80).
[2] A. Lods, *Israel*, E. T., p. 174; cf. Jack, *op. cit.*, Ch. II.
[3] Jack, *op. cit.*, Ch. XIII.
[4] See Ch. I, p. 8.

there was a relatively small group of people (not a district) somewhere in Palestine bearing the name 'Israel'. Similarly, there is evidence of another group called '*Asaru* in Western Galilee about 1313, who may be identified in name with the Hebrew tribe Asher.[1] Further, the place-names 'Ja'cob-el' and 'Joseph-el' are alleged to be found in the Karnak list of 1479 B.C.[2] These also, if correctly deciphered, might point to elements (or names) afterwards absorbed into the Israelite people (or tradition). The archaeological evidence for an early date for the Exodus is often presented as more convincing than it is. Archaeologists are by no means agreed as to Garstang's date of 1407 for the destruction of Jericho; Vincent puts it between 1250 and 1200; Ai seems to have been in ruins from 2000 to 1200 B.C.; Bethel seems to have been destroyed by fire between 1300 and 1250.[3] No firm argument can be drawn from the various chronological statements of the Old Testament. On the other hand, we have a list of eight Edomite kings (Gen. 36:31–39) down to David's conquest of Edom which appears to cover not much more than a couple of centuries from the period of the invasion; if so, this would date the beginning of the settlement in the thirteenth century.[4] Moreover, as against the identification of the Biblical invasion with that of the Ḥabiru in the fourteenth century, we note that the names of the four kings of Jerusalem, Lachish, Gezer and Hasor given in the Tell el-Amarna letters are quite different from those given in the Book of Joshua.[5] Even so brief a summary of the evidence as this suggests that it is not safe to abandon the direct Biblical evidence for a thirteenth-century date offered by Ex. 1:11.

[1] Burney, *Judges*, p. lxxxix.
[2] Burney, *op. cit.*, p. lxvii.
[3] A. Lods, *Archéologie et Ancien Testament*, in *Revue des Études Sémitiques*, 1936, pp. lix-lxiii.
[4] A. Lods, *Israel*, E. T., p. 185.
[5] Burney, *op. cit.*, p. cxvii.

3. The Work of Moses

Historically regarded, the oppression of Israel was the attempt to transform a relatively small and unimportant group of Bedouin, who had been allowed to settle in the pasture-lands of the eastern part of the Nile Delta (the western end of the Wady Tumilat), into state-slaves to be employed on public works. As a result of the leadership of Moses, these semi-nomads broke loose and resumed their former nomadic life. (A similar migration of Bedouin, refusing to be taxed by the Egyptian government, and from the same area, has occurred in modern times.[1]) In the Book of Exodus, these events are described as they appeared to the eyes of faith centuries afterwards. It is not necessary to recapitulate the familiar story, or to disentangle the three documents (J, E, P) from which the present narrative has been built up. But it is important for the history to know the significance of the work of Moses, however much or little of the detail of the present narrative be ascribed to his historic figure. He was not simply the leader of a successful revolt and escape from oppression; he was also a prophet,[2] in the sense that he gave a supernatural interpretation to what others might have regarded as natural happenings. We are never likely to know what these were, and are left to conjecture. A recent writer,[3] for example, has found an explanation of both the plagues of Egypt and the crossing of the Red Sea in a widespread volcanic and seismic upheaval. A simpler explanation of the crossing is that of Ex. 14:21: 'Yahweh caused the sea to go back by a strong east wind all the night, and made the sea dry land, and the waters were divided.' The point of real importance is that whatever happened was interpreted by Moses as the work of Yahweh, the future God of Israel. Here we have that mingling of the

---

[1] Driver, *Exodus*, p. lvi.

[2] Dt. 18:15; 34:10; cf. Ex. 33:11; Num. 12:6–8; and the narrative of his 'call' in Ex. 3.

[3] W. J. Phythian-Adams, *The Call of Israel*, pp. 155 ff.

event with its religious interpretation, to constitute the fact for faith, which characterizes the history of Israel as recorded in the Old Testament. Moses was doing essentially what Isaiah did in the times of Sennacherib, when he bade the people look beyond the outer deliverance to its inner meaning: 'ye looked not unto Him that had done this, neither had ye respect unto Him that fashioned it long ago.' (Is. 22:11.) Israel's faith was created by an act of divine redemption, i.e., by the interpretation of that act as the work of Yahweh: 'Israel saw the great work which Yahweh did upon the Egyptians, and the people feared Yahweh: and they had faith in Yahweh and in Moses His servant.' (Ex. 14:31.) The ancient song of Miriam (Ex. 15:21) takes us to the heart of this faith:

Sing ye to Yahweh, for He hath triumphed gloriously;
The horse and his rider hath He thrown into the sea.

The overthrow of Egypt holds a place in the religion of Israel which may be compared with that of the victory of the Cross for the Christian. Here was that mighty act of God to which faith could ever return for its renewal. Here began the divine 'election' of Israel, the consciousness of which characterizes the Old Testament from beginning to end, and continues to form the inspiration of Judaism. The literary evidence suggests that this doctrine of election was based on the Exodus in the first place, and only subsequently was carried back to the patriarchs.[1]

In the light of this conviction ('I will take you to me for a people, and I will be to you a God', Ex. 6:7), we gain our surest clue to the ultimate distinction of the religion of Israel from all its contemporary religions, such as Moab's faith in Kemosh. Yahweh is no nature-God, like those Baalim of Canaan whom He will ultimately overcome, though He thunders from Sinai, and can come in storm to the help of His hard-pressed people.[2] From the outset of His historic

---

[1] K. Galling, *Die Erwählungstraditionen Israels*, p. 63.
[2] Cf. Judges 5:20, 21, etc.

relation to Israel, He is characterized by this initial choice of them, which is a moral act. Here is the germ of that unique correlation of morality and religion which was to bear its noble fruit in the prophets. Here is the secret of their strange ability to reinterpret even national disaster in terms of a divine purpose. In this sense, Moses is the human founder of the religion of Israel. He taught that Yahweh had chosen this group of tribes by delivering them from Egypt, and Yahweh was to be henceforth the only God of Israel. By the side of this primary contribution, all others that he may have made to moral and religious legislation are secondary. The picture of him as law-giver in the primitive sense, to be found in Ex. 18, is doubtless true to history, though even the Decalogue may be a later summary of the prophetic religion of the eighth century.

The exact route taken by the Israelites under the leadership of Moses cannot be traced; even if the place-names are taken as accurate they cannot be located. But they passed into the desert east of Egypt, ultimately reaching 'the wilderness of Sinai' (Ex. 19:1). This has been traditionally located, since the fourth century A.D., in the so-called Sinaitic peninsula, between the Gulf of Suez on the west and the Gulf of Akaba on the east. One of the highest mountains there is Jebel Musa, the traditional Sinai (7,636 ft.), almost at the centre of the peninsula. In the judgment of many scholars, however, Sinai must have been somewhere in the neighbourhood of Kadesh (fifty miles south of Beersheba), which the Israelites seem to have made their real centre during the wilderness period. This is the country of the Amalekites, a Bedouin tribe of the desert south of Palestine, with whom Israel fought (Ex. 17:8–16). Others have argued that Sinai lay rather to the east of the Gulf of Akaba, that country being the proper home of the Midianites, the tribe into which Moses married. But wherever Sinai lay, it was the chief scene of the religious experience mediated by Moses which made Yahweh the God of Israel and Israel the people of Yahweh. The great mass of the legislation, and perhaps all of it, ascribed to this event in the Pentateuch demonstrably belongs to later periods of the nation's history. The historic events must have been of much simpler character, though they may well have included some form of 'covenant' (*berith*), expressing the love (*hesed*) out of which sprang Yahweh's choice of Israel. The Mosaic Yahweh is described as a localized God, linked specially to Sinai, a God of storm and battle, and a giver of oracles (Kadesh, the 'sacred' place). The fact that He would tolerate no other God for Israel did not prevent the Israelites from recognizing that there were other gods for other peoples.

That Yahweh was closely connected with Sinai, 'the mountain of God' (Ex. 3:1), is clear from many indications, and most explicitly from Dt. 33:2:

> Yahweh came from Sinai,
>> And beamed forth from Seir (Edom) unto them;
> He shined forth from mount Paran,
>> And came from Meribath-Kadesh.[1]

It has been conjectured that Yahweh was originally the God of Jethro, father-in-law to Moses, who was a priest of Midian, and took the lead in offering sacrifice (Ex. 18:12). The Kenites were a Midianite tribe, and they were on terms of friendship with Israel (Judges 1:16); their ancestor Kain (Cain) bore the Yahweh-mark, and the father-in-law of Moses is in one source described as a Kenite (Judges 4:11). We do not know with any certainty how far back the name 'Yahweh' may go; Assyriologists seem to be divided as to the recognition of the name in forms which occur from the time of Hammurabi.[2] But the mere occurrence of the name is of comparatively little significance, that which really matters is its connotation (etymology throws no light on the meaning). Just as Muhammad took the God Allah from the Arab pantheon, and exalted him to supreme, indeed to unique

---

[1] The last name as suggested by the LXX.
[2] G. R. Driver, in *ZAW*, 1928, p. 7, rejects any alleged occurrence before the ninth century B.C.

place, as the only true God, so Moses gave to the name Yahweh, whatever its previous history, a new significance for Israel. The Biblical tradition is itself inconsistent as to whether or not the name was previously known to Israel. According to the Priestly Code (Ex. 6:3), the name was now first revealed as something new: 'by my name Yahweh I was not known to (Abraham, Isaac and Jacob)'; the Elohist seems to agree, since he has previously avoided the use of the name. On the other hand, the Yahwist (Gen. 4:26) expressly declares that it was known to men from the earliest times.

4. THE INVASION OF CANAAN

According to the Biblical narrative *in its present form* (combined from at least three different documents), the Israelites, after leaving Sinai (Num. 10:12) under the guidance of the Ark (10:33–36),[1] tried to enter Canaan from the south, but were defeated at Hormah (14:45). They were refused a passage through the territory of Edom (20:14 ff.), so journeyed round it (21:4) to the east of the Jordan (21:13 ff.). Here they found that territory previously occupied by Moab and Ammon had been seized by the Amorites (Canaanites), whom Israel defeated at Yahaz in the south and Edrei in the north (21:23, 33). Most of the territory thus acquired from the Arnon to the Yarmuk was eventually occupied by the tribes called Reuben, Gad and Manasseh (in part). The main body of the Israelites forced their way into the heart of Canaan, the Josephites settling on the northern hills, with Shechem as their centre. A confederation of five 'kings' of southern Canaan (Josh 10) was decisively defeated in a single battle in the valley of Aijalon (*vv.* 12, 13), leading to the complete conquest of the south (*vv.* 40–43). A combination of four 'kings' in the north (11) was similarly defeated by the Waters of Merom. 'So', we read,

---

[1] 'Conceived of as moving by itself . . . Like the cloud, the ark moves because it is the form in which Yahweh accompanies the people' (G. B. Gray, *ad loc.*). The history of the Ark is an epitome of the earlier stages in the development of the religion.

C

'Joshua took the whole land . . . and gave it for an inheritance unto Israel according to their divisions by their tribes' (11:23).

This representation of a complete conquest in two great battles made by a solid body of the twelve tribes is, however, contradicted by the earlier strata of the combined narrative, as well as by the subsequent course of the history. The fragments of the Yahwistic writer (J) which are imbedded in the Book of Joshua tell us that Geshur and Maacath were not occupied by Israel (13:13); that Caleb, acting independently, took Hebron, and his ally, Othniel, took Debir (15:14–19); that Jerusalem remained in the hands of the Jebusites (15:63); that Gezer was not occupied (16:10), nor the line of important fortresses from Beth-shean across the valley of Jezreel and the plain of Esdraelon (Megiddo) westwards (17:11–13). The Josephites complain of being crowded into too narrow a territory by the Canaanites (17:14–18); Dan, similarly pressed, seeks new territory in the extreme north (19:47). Thus the earliest account of the 'Conquest' which we possess suggests that it was very partially achieved, and that, so far as it was achieved, it was the result of independent tribal warfare, rather than of a national invasion with conclusive campaigns under a single leader. In the narrative of Judges 1, we have another early document describing the piecemeal process of the settlement. Here we read of an independent invasion by Judah and Simeon (vv. 1–7), of Kenite movements from Jericho (16), of a Josephite occupation of the Bethel district (22–26), as well as of various tribal settlements amongst the Canaanite population. We know from the later history that the Canaanites were not exterminated, but gradually subjugated and absorbed. At first, by their superior organization and equipment, especially their war-chariots, they were able to retain the richest part of the country, viz., the plains, whilst the Israelites established themselves here and there in the hill country. The conquest of Canaan was in fact not completed until the time of David and Solomon; David was the first to conquer Jerusalem, and Solomon received Gezer from the Pharaoh who had conquered it.

There is similar misrepresentation of the constitution of Israel. When literature first recorded what had previously been but oral tradition, all the elements of the then-existent Israel had to be accounted for; hence the theory of the twelve tribes descended from the twelve sons of Jacob. The stories told of these sons often seem to reflect the ancient traditions of tribal or clan movements. Thus, the story of Simeon and Levi treacherously destroying Shechemites on account of their sister Dinah,[1] and of the alarm of Jacob at the opposition which this aroused amongst the Canaanites (Gen. 34), may really record the events which led to the disappearance of Levi as a secular clan, and the practical absorption of Simeon in Judah (cf. Gen. 49:5–7). The curious and repellent story of Judah's union with his Canaanite daughter-in-law, Tamar, may record the fact that Judah absorbed many native elements into its tribal life. It seems probable, indeed, that 'Judah', or rather the nucleus of the future Judah, entered Canaan from the south, and not (as is represented even in Judges 1) from Jericho. We saw that one narrative (Num. 14:45) represented the Israelites as being *defeated* at Hormah. But another (Num. 21:3) represents them as being victorious over the Canaanites at the same place, and this is corroborated by Judges 1:17. Further, we find that in the genealogy of 1 Chron. 2, the descendants of Judah are made to include the Jerahmeelites (v. 9), and the Kenites (v. 55) who were north Arabian nomads, and that Caleb is elsewhere called a Kenizzite (Josh 14:6, etc.), the tribe Kenaz being Edomite (Gen. 36:11). It is at first sight strange that the tribe of Judah, which much later became the heir and upholder of Yahwism, should have been of the most mixed racial origin, though it may usefully remind us that

[1] See Appendix II, for the early clan of 'Dinah', perhaps absorbed by the Shechemites long before the descendants of these were themselves absorbed in Israel. For the close relations of Israelites and Shechemites, cf. the story of Abimelech (Judges 9).

nationality is not to be identified with race. But at the time
of which we are now thinking, the future lay with the Joseph
tribes who had been led from Egypt to Kadesh and Sinai by
Moses, and thence to the east of Jordan. These were to be
the nucleus of the Israelites of the future, and to be this by
virtue of their faith in Yahweh, which was the dominant
factor in creating and unifying the nation. Without them
and the faith they brought, those elements of the future
Israel which may have already settled in Canaan—i.e., all
except the Josephite (Rachel) tribes—would doubtless have
been absorbed into the Canaanite stock, or remained for us,
like their kinsfolk the Edomites, the Ammonites and the
Moabites, little more than names occurring from time to time
on the monuments of their Assyrian or Egyptian conquerors.

The Song of Deborah, probably the earliest written source
(c. 1100) for the history of Israel which we possess, is of
particular value in confirming our general conclusions as to
the true nature of the settlement in Canaan. It is a brilliant
and contemporaneous 'Te Deum' of victory, won by a group
of Israelite tribes in the north of Canaan over the Canaanite
inhabitants of the great Plain of Megiddo. It shows us the
Israelites in possession of the hill-country north and south
of the Plain, which the Canaanites are able to dominate by
their fortified cities and their war-chariots. Their combination against the Israelites is met by the war-cry of Deborah
the prophetess, who rouses some, but not all, of the Israelites
to face the crisis in the Israelite settlement caused by this
combination. We see the battle rolling down the valley of
the Kishon, and the swollen river helping the Israelites, since
'the stars in their courses (supposed to control the weather)
fought against Sisera'. We see Sisera himself, the leader of
the enemy, slain by the patriotic Jael, when he has taken
refuge as a fugitive in her tent. The poem closes with the
unforgettable picture of the mother of Sisera looking from
the window for the return of her son from his expected
victory, and speculating on the spoil which he will surely win
from Israel. We notice that the one centre around which the

tribes of Israel rally is their war-god Yahweh, who has come
to their help in this time of great need from His ancient shrine
at Sinai.

5. THE PERIOD OF THE 'JUDGES'

Our reference to the Song of Deborah has already brought
us into the period between the first Israelite invasions and
the point at which Saul emerges to take that militant kingship which David transformed into a regular monarchy, a
period of perhaps a couple of centuries. The period can be
conveniently called by the name of our one direct source for
it, viz., the Book of Judges. But we must beware of mis-
reading the term. These 'judges' are not primarily judicial
or magisterial figures; they are not even national figures.
They are more or less localized heroes or 'saviours' (2:16),
who have been much later fitted into the scheme of recurrent
phases of sin, punishment, penitence and deliverance by
which the writers we call 'Deuteronomistic' (c. 600) interpreted the past history (this philosophy of history is explicitly
given in 2:18–22). The scheme treats these heroes as if, like
David and Solomon, they ruled over a united country. Yet
the actual stories of these men show them to have been of
much more limited and local significance, and some of them
may easily have been contemporaries. We saw, from the
Song of Deborah, how Deborah and Barak gathered a
number of the northern tribes together to fight against the
Canaanites. The very conditions of this effort show that it
was something quite unusual. The southern tribes, Judah,
Simeon and Levi, are not named, and may not have been in
existence at this time, Simeon and Levi having been virtually
exterminated and Judah not yet recognized as an Israelite
tribe—though distance from the scene of operations in the
north may also account for the silence about them. Reuben
and Gad (Gilead), the tribes across the Jordan, are blamed
for their failure to unite with the rest, as are Dan and Asher,
the latter evidently living in close relations with the neighbouring Canaanites, which they are reluctant to break. Thus

the greatest united act of which we know in this period is very far from being that of a permanently united people. This feature is even more clearly illustrated by the other stories. Samson's exploits occur in a small district of S.W. Canaan, the original home of the Danites. Gideon delivers and for a time rules over a limited area of central Canaan. Some of the names seem to be merely schematic, and nothing is told about them; of the rest, we remember Jephthah in connection with his ill-fated daughter, Gideon for his battle-cry and picked warriors, Abimelech for his slaughter of his seventy brethren, Ehud for his treacherous assassination of the king of Moab.

Some of the stories show the continuance of that pressure from the east which constantly brought nomads or semi-nomads into the more settled lands. In some such westward 'drive', the Moabites, with the help of the Ammonites and the Amalekites, had captured Jericho; this led Ehud to assassinate Eglon the Moabite king, to gather the Ephraimites and to seize the fords of the Jordan. In the same way, Jephthah's importance lay in delivering his own fellow-Gileadites from the pressure of the Ammonites (Judges 11), though himself an outlaw. Again, we see the Midianites (found in both the south and the east) occupying the territory of Manasseh, until Gideon of that tribe led the Israelites of the centre and north against them (6ff.). Gideon himself to some degree and for a short time anticipated Saul's kingship. His half-breed son, Abimelech, with the help of the Shechemites, to whom he was related through his mother, murdered the other descendants of Gideon, and maintained himself as a petty king for three years (9:22), his domain being probably from the plain of Megiddo to Shechem. When a certain Gaal stirred up the Shechemites against him, he attacked Abimelech as being an Israelite (9:28f.). The ambiguous position of such a half-breed is doubtless typical of many in this transitional period.

When we try to reconstruct the life of the Israelites at this time, the most important and influential fact is the change from the nomadic to the settled and agricultural mode of life. When the nomadic clan settles down, many changes will naturally ensue. Property will become the basis of organization, and the elders will constitute their court of appeal at the gate of the town. New occupations—the culture of olive, fig and vine, the growth of corn, the development of the arts of the potter, the weaver and the smith, trade by barter and consequent increase in intercourse with other groups—all these imply or lead to a different kind of life. The Israelites found the Canaanites already in possession of this much higher stage of civilization, and naturally took over their acquisitions. It is significant, and a further confirmation of what has been said about the gradual character of the settlement, that archaeology offers no evidence of a marked break between Canaanite and Israelite periods of culture, such as a complete conquest might have afforded. The relations of the Israelites with the Canaanites would naturally vary in different areas—in some they were conquerors, in others equals, and in others they were doubtless themselves absorbed.[1] These changes would be gradual, as the Israelites came down from the hill country to mingle in the life of the strong towns of the Canaanites. In some cases, the Israelites failed to make good their position, and had to migrate, as happened to the Danites.

The religion of the times is best illustrated by a pair of pictures. One is that given in the narrative of Shiloh and the child Samuel, representing one of the more important sanctuaries; the other, that of the entertainment of Saul and his servant by Samuel at one of the 'high places' (1 Sam. 9) showing the religious observance at a smaller place. The communion feast was an important feature in both (as we may infer for Shiloh from Eli's suspicion that Hannah was drunk). There were festivals at the vintage (Jud. 9:27) and at the sheep-shearing (Nabal, 1 Sam. 25:7). In the sacrifices, the head of the family would naturally act as 'priest'; the blood would be poured out on some sacred rock or stone

[1] As, possibly, the lost clan of Dinah (see p. 25n).

(1 Sam. 14:33 ff.). It may have been from the Canaanites that the Hebrews learnt to burn the fat to the deity. A rich man, such as Micah (Jud. 17) might hire a professional priest; the whole story of Micah's Levite told in this connection is a highly suggestive one for the religious and social conditions of the time. The Book of the Covenant,[1] though probably first compiled under the early monarchy, is another rich source of information, as reflecting the new kind of life resulting from the settlement in Canaan.

In recent years attention has increasingly been focused on the possibility that the Israelite confederacy of twelve tribes echoed a prevailing pattern of tribal organization in ancient times. It is termed 'amphictyonic' since in Greece the term 'amphictyony' was used to describe a twelve-tribe organization centring on a particular shrine and maintaining the customs of that shrine. The central sacred object of the Israelite 'amphictyony' was probably the Ark. There may also have been six-tribe amphictyonies. It is possible that one such had its centre at Shechem and another in the south at Hebron. Although the central shrine would not exclude the existence of other shrines and centres of worship, the fact that there had been a central shrine at some stage in Israel's history made possible the future development of Israel's one-sanctuary tradition and worship.

[1] i.e. Exod. 20:22–23:19.

III.—THE EARLY MONARCHY

1. THE PHILISTINES

THE Exodus from Egypt gave Israel a religion; the settlement in Canaan gave them a land; the pressure of the Philistines gave them a king. The Philistines occupied the maritime plain between Judah and the sea, separated from the Judaean hills by the Shephelah, or 'foot-hills', and extending over some forty miles of coast from Joppa in the north to the south of Gaza; at one time they also occupied the plain of Esdraelon and the valley of Jezreel to Beth-shean. They were without the harbours which made the Phoenicians north of Carmel into a seafaring people, but they had a rich soil, and were astride the great coast-road which led to the north and east. Whence and when did they come?

About 1200 B.C. the Egyptian Pharaoh, Rameses III, was attacked from the Syrian side by 'the peoples of the sea', themselves possibly forced to seek new settlements through the pressure of northern hordes of Aryans. These sea-peoples seem to have been largely Aegean, and included tribes called the Pulusatu (known to us as the Philistines), and the Zekal of Zakkala. They overran North Syria, breaking up the Hittite power there. Rameses defeated them by land and sea on and off the coast of Phoenicia, but apparently allowed them to settle on the coast of Southern Syria, since we find the Zekal round about Dor, south of Carmel, and the Pulusatu still further south.[1] The features and attire of these Philistines, as depicted on the Egyptian monuments, are neither Egyptian nor Semitic, but apparently link them with the

[1] The references to the Philistines in the patriarchal stories (e.g., Gen. 26:1), as settled in Palestine before this date, are of course anachronistic.

31

early pre-Greek peoples of the coasts of Asia Minor, the
Aegean, Crete and Cyprus, and the pottery found in the ruins
of Philistine cities seems to confirm this. The Old Testament
says that the Philistines came from Caphtor, which may be
Crete: cf. Amos 9:7, Jer. 47:4, Dt. 2:23.

The Philistines probably brought with them into the land
to which they were to give their name—'Palestine'—a good
deal of the pre-Greek (late Minoan) culture, and they are by
no means to be regarded as 'barbarians', in spite of the
modern use of their name in this sense. The Aegean influences
had operated in Canaan long before the coming of the
Philistines, though the Philistines doubtless reinforced those
influences.[1] We cannot test their racial origin by language,
for we know nothing of this, but it is significant that the
Israelites designate them as 'uncircumcised' (1 Sam. 18:25),
a term which marks them off from both Semites and
Egyptians. The Philistines, like the Hebrews, seem to have
adopted the customs and language of the Canaanites. Their
deities were Semitic, e.g., Dagon the corn-god, Atargatis of
Ashkelon, an equivalent of Astarte, Baal-zebub of Ekron.[2]
The well-known federation of the five cities, each under a
seren (or 'tyrant'), viz., Ekron, Ashdod, Ashkelon, Gaza and
Gath (e.g., Josh 13:3), points to closer co-operation than was
usual amongst the Canaanites. Their land was one of the
most fertile parts of western Palestine.

The Philistine invaders of Canaan had come to stay, for
they had brought with them their families and possessions
in heavy two-wheeled ox-carts, as the Egyptian records show
us. They came, as did the Israelite invaders contemporary

---

[1] Macalister, in his Schweich Lectures on the Philistines (p. 123),
remarks: 'the impression which the daily study of objects found in
excavation has made on the present writer is, that from about 1400–1200
B.C. onwards to about 800 B.C. Western Palestine was the scene of a
struggle between the Aegean and Egyptian civilizations, with a slight
mingling of Mesopotamian influence, and that the local tribes [i.e., the
Canaanites and Israelites] took a merely passive interest in the conflict
and made no contribution whatever to its development.' (Cf. Lods,
Israel, E.T., p. 70.)

[2] Possibly the 'Beelzebul' of Matt. 10:25 (R.V. *mar.*).

with them, at a time of opportunity. From the end of the reign of Rameses III, i.e., from the earlier half of the twelfth century down to the middle of the ninth century, when the Assyrians began seriously to threaten Canaan, the country was left more or less free from foreign interference. The Canaanites themselves lacked cohesion both in the Amarna period and in the period of the settlement of the Israelites. The result was that the control of Canaan lay open to the hands of either Israel or of the Philistines, and it was the Philistines who first asserted themselves against an Israel which had not yet found its unity and strength.

Our first record of contact between the Philistines and Israel is in the Samson-stories of Judges 13–16. The Danites, the tribe to which Samson belonged, were settled about Zorah and Eshtaol, which were in the Shephelah due east of Jerusalem. The Philistines were clearly stronger than their neighbours and could dictate to them and to the men of Judah, which is what we should expect from their superior military equipment and experience (cf. 15:11: 'Knowest thou not that the Philistines are rulers over us?').

The first fighting between the Philistines and the Israelites is that recorded in 1 Sam. 4–7, which led to the Philistine conquest of the central portion of the land, occupied by Ephraim and Benjamin. Israel was defeated in the first attack, but essayed a second battle, this time bringing with them the Ark from Shiloh, with its two priests, Hophni and Phinehas. The object was, of course, to enlist Yahweh, the God of the Ark, more actively on their side. But after the first dismay of the Philistines, the device proved disastrous, for Israel was again defeated, and the Ark was captured. This could mean only that Yahweh had abandoned Israel, or was powerless before their enemies, and the shock of the news killed the aged Eli. The Ark, however, itself proved an embarrassment to its captors; its presence at Ashdod and Gath was accompanied by pestilence, and Ekron refused to receive it. Finally the Ark was returned to Israel, with an atoning offering to the wronged God whom it represented.

But even when it reached Beth-shemesh, the first Israelite town, misfortune accompanied it, and the people there passed it on to Kiriath-jearim, the next place in the valley that leads up towards Jerusalem. Here it remained for twenty years. In all probability, its original home, Shiloh, had been destroyed by the Philistines, though no record of this has been kept in the present context. But we have a later reference to its destruction in Jer. 7:12–14:

> But go ye now unto my place which was in Shiloh, where I caused my name to dwell at the first, and see what I did to it for the wickedness of my people Israel.

According to 1 Sam. 7:5–14, this defeat was followed by a miraculous victory over the Philistines, won through the intercession of Samuel, and so complete that 'the Philistines were subdued and they came no more within the border of Israel' (v. 13); but this is utterly inconsistent with the whole subsequent history, and the life-work of Saul and of David. Samuel is a sufficiently important figure to be able to dispense with this unhistorical glorification of his service.

2. SAMUEL AND SAUL

It was Samuel who took the momentous step of introducing the kingship into Israel, with a view to meeting the national peril from the Philistines. It is difficult for the ordinary reader to form a clear picture of the personality of Samuel, largely because the Bible includes documents from different sources, showing an inconsistent attitude towards the monarchy. According to the earlier and much more credible source (9, 10:1–16, 11:1–11, 15), Samuel is a seer or prophet, in some connection with the bands of wandering prophets who appear at this time, though he is evidently far above them in personality and outlook. They are represented as coming down from the high place with a psaltery and a timbrel and a pipe and a harp, and 'prophesying' in such a way that their ecstatic condition can be contagious (10:5; cf. 19:18–24). Samuel's first choice of a king was a man psychically susceptible to this contagion, though possessing other qualities of physique and courage and leadership, which marked him out as the fighting captain whom the Israelites needed against the Philistines. The combination of qualities suggests that Samuel hoped for a prophet-king, as Plato for a philosopher-king; at any rate this psychic susceptibility explains much in the more sombre aspects of Saul, and the extremes to which his jealousy of David was to urge him. In this earlier narrative, Saul is secretly anointed king by Samuel and bidden to watch his opportunity of coming forward. This came a month later (R.V. *mar.* of 1 Sam. 10:27), when the people of Jabesh-Gilead across the Jordan sent an appeal for help against the cruelty of the Ammonites. Saul is seized by a psychic frenzy at the news, and by a piece of 'prophetic symbolism' summons the Israelites, and leads them to victory against the Ammonites. The outcome of this deed is that Saul is publicly recognized as king in Gilgal.[1]

The other narrative, which is interwoven with this in our present text (7, 8, 10:17–24), represents Samuel as a 'judge' of Israel, who opposes the demand of the people for a king, and warns them of his future tyranny and oppression, in terms that suggest a long experience of the kingship. He yields, however, to their demand, and Saul is chosen by lot, and elected king at Mizpah. The interest of this narrative is not in regard to the alleged events, but in regard to the later attitude of Hosea and his school to the kingship in Israel, which it apparently reflects. Hosea's attitude to the monarchy is emphatically hostile, and it must be admitted that his experience of the northern kings in the last half-century of Israel's history gave him good ground for his hostility (Hos. 8:4; 13:10, 11). This attitude should be remembered, in contrast to that idealization of the kingship which eventually led to the 'Messianic' hope.

Samuel's subsequent disappointment with the man of his

[1] Another view is that the opportunity came when Saul overthrew the Philistine garrison at Gibeah, see A. Lods: *Israel*, p. 352.

own choice seems to be reflected in two narratives which each describe an open breach between the two men. In 1 Sam. 13:8–14, on the eve of hostilities against the Philistines, Saul offers the customary sacrifices, after long waiting for Samuel to do this; Samuel then appears and treats this as an act of disobedience to Yahweh, for which the penalty will be the loss of the kingdom in favour of another. In 15:10–31, Saul fails to put the Amalekites to the ban of destruction, sparing Agag the king and the best of the cattle for sacrifice, and Samuel again denounces Saul as abandoned by Yahweh ('to obey is better than sacrifice and to hearken than the fat of rams', 22). Whatever historic truth may lie behind such narratives as these, they do seem to show that Saul failed to be the prophet-king for whom Samuel had hoped, and that the unity of the sacred and the secular arms was not attained by the first kingship of Israel.

We must not fail to recognize, however, the importance of the step taken by Samuel in initiating a kingship in Israel, and the historical significance of Samuel himself. Guthe has pointed out[1] that 'history and legend bring Samuel forward in all the rôles which were possible for an outstanding man of those times—as seer, as Nazirite, as priest, as judge, and as prophet—a clear proof that in the time between Moses and the monarchy no man was known of equal importance for Israel'. To us the chief justification for this must be that the establishment of the monarchy with all its consequences, secular and religious, was due to Samuel. There had been already an attempt at a more or less local kingship by Abimelech; but Samuel's was national and in the national interest, even though Saul's immediate following was made up of his own Benjamite tribesmen, and his *ménage* and court were of the simplest. The 'kingship' of the Canaanites was territorial, not national.[2] Moreover, the Israelite kingship illustrates another important feature; it involved election by the people, even though this was more or less dominated by

[1] *Geschichte des Volkes Israel*,[3] p. 83.
[2] Galling, *Israelitische Staatsverfassung*, p. 15.

hereditary succession. This is seen in the attitude of the
Israelites to Rehoboam after the death of Solomon, and it is
seen particularly in the south, when Joash and Josiah, both
minors, came to the throne.[1] We see it also in regard to the
legislation. Whilst, as in the whole of the ancient East, this
is regarded as of divine origin, it is through the confirmation
by the people (by means of a covenant) that it first acquires
juristic authority.[2] Attention has rightly been called to the
importance of this feature of the Israelite kingship, in contrast
with that of surrounding peoples. 'Israel—the one genuine
Palestinian nation of ancient times—must receive the credit
for one of the greatest contributions ever made to the political
thought of man. She brought with her from the nomad stage
a conception of common brotherhood which she was the first
to apply to the conditions of a highly organized settled
community. . . . Except in her conception of religion Israel
had no greater gift to offer to the world than this, a truly
democratic theory of the relation between the government
and the governed.'[3]

The reign of Saul was chiefly absorbed in military operations, primarily[4] against the Philistines (1 Sam. 14:52), for
this was the task which called him to the kingship, and the
task handed on to his successor. The Philistine domination
seems to have been complete at the outset of his reign, as we
may judge from the disarmament of the Israelites (13:19f.)
and from the reference to a Philistine 'prefect' (nesib 13:3;
so in 10:5, rather than 'garrison') in Geba or Gibeah, the city
of Saul himself (11:4), opposite to Michmash. It was here
that Jonathan, the daring son of Saul, gave the signal for
revolt by killing the Philistine prefect (13:3). The Philistines
brought up their troops and faced Saul with his small army
of six hundred men—all that remained faithful in face of

---

[1] Op. cit., p. 32.   [2] Ex. 24:3; 2 Kings 23:3; Neh. x:28 ff.
[3] T. H. Robinson, in his Schweich lecture (Palestine in General
History, pp. 41–44).
[4] Cf. 1 Sam. 14:47 f., for his success against Moabites, Ammonites,
Edomites and Aramaeans; reference has been made to a campaign
against the Amalekites.

great peril—across the valley from Michmash, the valley of the Suweinit, opening eastwards to Jordan. The Philistines sent out raiding parties. It was Jonathan who again took the initiative against them, by climbing the rocks opposite with his armour-bearer and against all expectation driving out the enemy's advanced post. Saul's sentries on the opposite hills reported what was happening, though its cause was unknown, and Saul with his troops now joined in the battle, reinforced by other Israelites when they saw the promise of victory. Jonathan narrowly escaped death, not from the enemy who were defeated, but from his unwitting breach of a taboo.

Apart from the final scene on Gilboa, the only other battle of which we have particulars is that in the Valley of Elah, south-west of Jerusalem in the Shephelah, on the opposite side of the central range. This is the battle containing the less likely of the two accounts of David's introduction to Saul, namely, that through his slaughter of Goliath (17). The more likely alternative is that of the previous chapter (16:14–23), according to which David was chosen to be king's minstrel. The subsequent relations between Saul and David are not easy to follow in detail, partly owing to duplicate narratives, but the general course is clear enough. David's personal courage and striking personality made him a *persona grata* at court, the intimate friend of the king's son, the king's son-in-law, and his most likely successor. This aroused the jealousy of Saul's darkened spirit, and led him to attempt the life of his best captain, at a time when he needed all the help he could get against the enemy. David took to flight and became an outlaw in the country round Hebron, collecting there a band of freebooters. Even this did not secure him from the relentless pursuit of Saul, and David found it necessary to take refuge with the Philistines themselves.[1]

The battle of Gilboa was fought on the hills south of the Valley of Jezreel. The Philistines remained in control of this valley and of Esdraelon all the days of Saul, and in Saul's final campaign they seem to have been attacking the central

[1] 21: 10–15, the story of his feigned madness, seems a late 'Midrash'.

range from this northern point. They gathered in Aphek,
i.e., probably in the Sharon district, moved into Esdraelon
by one of the passes, perhaps that of Megiddo, and took up
their position at Shunem (28:4; this chapter should follow 29
and precede 31, as it describes the visit to Endor the night
before the battle). Saul and three of his sons were killed
(leaving only Ishbaal) and the Israelites were disastrously
defeated. The Philistines sent Saul's head and armour for
exhibition in their cities, whilst they hung up his body and
the bodies of his sons in Beth-shean. Saul's task thus ended
in tragic failure, tragic in the deeper sense of character, as
well as in that of circumstance.

3. DAVID

With David, the historian enters upon a period in which
he may tread with firmer footing. The literary data[1] are
ampler and more reliable; the interest in David created
contemporary records for some of the most important events
of his life.

David's career falls into three main divisions, viz., his life
prior to the death of Saul up to the age of thirty (1 Sam.
15–31), the seven and a half years during which he was king
of Judah and subsequently (five years in all) king also of
Israel in Hebron (2 Sam. 1–5:3), and the thirty-three years
(2 Sam. 5:4, 5) during which he was king of Israel and of
Judah at Jerusalem, i.e., c. 40 in all (2 Sam. 5:4) for his
reign. According to the earlier and more reliable narrative
(1 Sam. 16:14–23), David was introduced to Saul on account
of his musical skill, in order to drive away the fits of melan-
cholia that troubled Saul. David was however, at this time,
reported as not only 'cunning in playing', but also 'a mighty
man of valour, and a man of war, and prudent in speech, and
a comely person'. With such an equipment, he speedily
became a popular figure, and was made the king's armour-

---

[1] The general attitude of the present writer to the historical value of
the Old Testament is indicated briefly in 'The Old Testament: its Making
and Meaning', Ch. III.

D

bearer, became the bosom-friend of the king's son, and married the king's daughter, Michal. Saul, however, had become jealous of one whom the panegyric of oriental exaggeration accounted a better soldier than himself:

> 'Saul hath slain his thousands,
> And David his ten thousands'

the women sang. Saul, therefore, seems to have made the gift of Michal conditional on an apparently impossible military task, and was greatly chagrined when David escaped unhurt, with increased renown. David's life was threatened, and he escaped only through a device of his wife. Flight meant that he was an outlaw, and the help he obtained by misrepresentation from Ahimelech the priest (21) led to the massacre of eighty-five members of the priestly community at Nob. David put his parents into the custody of the king of Moab, and himself became a hunted fugitive. We read of his adventures in different places of refuge in the south— Keilah, Ziph, Carmel, En-gedi, Adullam. He gathered round him the inevitable circle of the discontented and the out-lawed, besides his own kin, and this formed the nucleus of a fighting force. For the present, he was simply a freebooter, protecting more settled folk from other marauders in return for the toll he exacted. A characteristic incident of this period is the story of Nabal, who refused to pay his toll, and escaped from David's impulsive wrath only through the shrewdness of his wife, Abigail, whose eventual marriage to David must have added greatly to his resources. Subsequently, David found it necessary to take refuge further afield, with the enemies of his people. Here he played a double part, avoiding attack on Israelites, whilst leading the Philistines to regard him as their ally, though naturally one subject to suspicion. Fortunately for David's future plans, he was not allowed to accompany the Philistine host which defeated Saul at Gilboa; David found enough to do meantime in a campaign of vengeance against the Amalekites, southern Bedouin who had raided Ziklag, David's headquarters. The policy of David, and the ambitions he was already cherishing, are shown by his distribution of the spoil won on this campaign amongst certain cities of Judah, which he evidently wished to attach to himself (30:26ff.). The news of the death of Saul and Jonathan marks the close of the first period of David's public life. The elegy which he composed on that event (2 Sam. 1:19–27) shows the generosity of spirit which was one of his characteristics.

The second period begins with the recognition of David as king of Judah in Hebron. His policy is again shown by his prompt recognition of the respect exhibited by the men of Jabesh-gilead towards the insulted bodies of Saul and his sons (2 Sam. 2:5; cf. 1 Sam. 31:11f.). But several years were to pass before the policy of winning the northern half of the people could take effect. Abner, who was Saul's first cousin and his commander-in-chief, was 'carrying on' in the name of Saul's weak son, Ishbaal, at Mahanaim, in the district east of Jordan, whilst the Philistines occupied central Palestine. David followed a waiting policy, and eventually circumstances played into his hands, for Abner quarrelled with the titular king, Ishbaal, about the ownership of Rizpah, one of Saul's harem, and as a result made overtures to David, who was only waiting for some such opportunity. David's pacific policy was interrupted rudely by the jealous Joab, his own right-hand man, who had a blood-feud with Abner. The treacherous murder of Abner by Joab was the occasion of another genuine fragment of David's poetry:

Was it a fool's death that Abner was to die?
Thy hands were not bound, and thy feet were not put into
    fetters;
As a man falls before the unjust, thou hast fallen.
                    (2 Sam. 3:33, 34)

The death of Abner, Ishbaal's strength, led directly to Ishbaal's assassination by two men seeking to curry favour with David. The inevitable course of accepting David's kingship over all Israel was now adopted by the representatives of the north, who came to Hebron (2 Sam. 5:3). Since this would be soon after the death of Ishbaal, who reigned for two years after the death of Saul (2 Sam. 2:10), there is a space of five years during which David was king over both Judah and Israel in Hebron, before he captured Jerusalem. During these years we must put his struggle against the Philistines.

The Philistines were not likely to accept without resistance a reunion of the divided and hitherto helpless forces of Judah and Israel. David defeated them in two battles in the valley of Rephaim (5:17–25), south-west of Jerusalem. This is stated almost summarily, but the exploits of David's warriors told in the appendix to the book (2 Sam. 21:15–22; 23:8–39), that of bringing the water of the well of Bethlehem, and many another, seem to have belonged to this time; the struggle was so severe that we read of David being forced again into his former stronghold of Adullam (23:13). But eventually, the Philistine peril was removed forever, the peril which had threatened the very existence of Israel. The task which had proved too great for Saul's blind courage was accomplished by one who wedded shrewd policy to personal daring, and David succeeded where Saul had failed.

We pass to the third and most important period, to which the first and second were merely preparatory. The overthrow of the Philistines left David free to take the most important step of his reign, either from a political or a religious point of view, and that was to establish his capital at Jerusalem. Jerusalem appears in the Tell el-Amarna Letters of 1400, under the name 'Urusalim', as the fortified centre of a district. It was one of the Canaanite places which the invading Israelites were unable to reduce (Josh 15:63), and was called Jebus (Jud. 19:10). This was the mountain fortress which David captured against all expectation, so that it was henceforth known as the city of David (2 Sam. 5:9). The site appears to have been the southern part of the eastern hill (Ophel), which commands the one spring, Gihon. The political advantage of this capital for David was that it marked off the new period from that in which his

capital had been Hebron, and being neutral ground, between
Judah and Benjamin, commanding the main lines of communication between north and south, it was particularly
fitted for such a united and militant kingdom as that of
David. The fact that it was without religious traditions for
Israel was a gain, not a loss. For when David brought up
the venerable Ark to the 'City of David', the place acquired a
unique distinction, undisturbed by any previous associations,
a distinction which was destined to increase with the centuries
until the Deuteronomic legislation ultimately made Jerusalem
the only sanctuary. The possession of Jerusalem doubtless
contributed to the permanence of the Davidic dynasty in the
southern kingdom.

The narrative of the removal of the Ark to Jerusalem
throws light upon the religious ideas and customs of the time.
At the first attempt, the death of one of the attendants caused
such fear of it that it was deposited in the house of Obed-
edom,[1] for three months. As he was none the worse for it,
they tried again, and after a short experimental movement of
six paces, without disaster, David offered the sacrifice of an
ox and a fatling; this time the Ark was being carried on the
shoulders of men, instead of on a cart, as at first. It should be
noticed that David wore the primitive sacred garment (cf.
1 Sam. 2:18), the linen ephod (afterwards surviving as the
high priest's ephod), a short strip of cloth instead of the long
robe of the king, and that he offered the sacrifice, which was
illegal for him to do according to the (later) 'Law of Moses'.
The Chronicler, re-telling the story more than seven centuries
afterwards, is unable to conceive that a pious king like David
should have been guilty of such sacrilegious acts. He therefore characteristically edits the story, telling of David that
he did exactly what he ought to have done, in the light of
the Priestly Code (1 Chron. 16:40). David now wears a

[1] From Gath, and therefore a Philistine, probably belonging to
David's 'foreign' bodyguard of 'Cherethites and Pelethites' (2 Sam.
8:18). As Budde says, we may doubt whether any Israelite would have
undertaken so perilous a task. The Chronicler (1 Chron. 15:17, 18)
transforms Obed-edom into a Levite, to comply with the (later) Law.

processional robe, not simply a kilt (the kilt is mentioned in
1 Chron. 15:27, but it would be covered by the robe) and
the reason for his wife's indignation is suppressed. There is a
great company of priests and Levites, and only the Levites
are allowed to touch the Ark. The sacrifice, which they (not
David) offer, is seven times as great. Instead of the simple
horn as the one musical instrument of David's second
attempt, we hear of trumpets and lyres and harps and
cymbals. Obed-edom the Philistine is transformed into a
Levite, such as he ought to have been. Parts of Psalms 105,
106, which are anonymous in our Psalter, are here assigned
to David as ordained for the occasion. (A careful comparison
of the two narratives in 2 Sam. 6 and 1 Chron. 15, 16, will
usefully illustrate the development of the religious ritual of
Israel in the course of seven centuries.)

David considerably extended the Hebrew kingdom by
conquering and adding the territory of the Edomites, the
Moabites, the Ammonites on the east, and Zobah in the
north, and apparently even exacted tribute from Damascus
on the north-east, whilst he maintained friendly relations
with Hamath in the extreme north, with Phoenicia in the
north-west and (from the time of his victory over them)
with the Philistines on the west. It is very significant that
he drew his bodyguard, faithful through the dark days of
Absalom's rebellion, from the conquered Philistines. Such an
extensive kingdom naturally demanded and received some
development of organization, and it may have been in connection with this that David undertook that census which
was followed by a pestilence marking the displeasure of
Yahweh. The officers of the kingdom of whom we read
(2 Sam. 8:15–18) are Joab as commander-in-chief, Jehoshaphat the *mazkir*, or 'Recorder',[1] Zadok and Abiathar,[2] the
priests, David's sons being also priests, Seraiah the scribe or
'Secretary of State',[3] Benaiah the captain of the bodyguard,

[1] Perhaps a private secretary to the king, or, secretary of state.
[2] Read 'Abiathar the son of Ahimelech', with the Syriac; cf. 20:25.
[3] Or adjutant-general.

and Adoram (20:24) over the forced labour. David built himself a palace, with Hiram's aid (5:11, 12) and furnished it with the usual Oriental harem. It is in connection with this domestic side of David's life that the tragedy, or succession of tragedies, of his later years unfolds itself, making one of the most impressive moral studies which the Old Testament contains, all the more impressive because not told moralistically, but with naïve realism. The story of David and Bathsheba is one of low and treacherous cunning, as well as unrestrained lust, and this dark background is only partially redeemed by the behaviour of the king when he suffers the loss of his child. We see the father's lust repeated in the rape of Tamar by Amnon, David's eldest son, a misdeed which David does not punish, however angry he may be. The sequel of this is Amnon's murder by Absalom, Absalom's flight and alienation from David, followed by Absalom's rebellion and death, and the bitter sorrow of David, who probably saw himself most fully in Absalom. The third episode in this great moral drama is the attempt of Adonijah to claim the crown from his aged and failing father (1 Kings 1). It is significant that Adonijah had the support of most of the court, but the prompt action of Nathan, Zadok, Benaiah and the bodyguard secured the election of Solomon the son of Bathsheba. There is far more dignity in Saul's end than in David's.

We notice in the events following Absalom's rebellion the evidence of division between the northern and southern tribes, never absent although concealed during the reigns of David and Solomon. After the death of Absalom, for which David never forgave Joab, David made overtures to Amasa, Absalom's commander-in-chief, and promised him Joab's place, with the result that Joab took the first opportunity of killing Amasa. Joab then stamped out the revolt of a Benjamite named Sheba, who had appealed to the fact that David was a Judaean, and endeavoured to arouse the old tribal animosities. It should be said that David, either by policy or fortune, was free throughout from any peril from

Saul's kinsmen. Seven of them had been hung up before
Yahweh, to break a famine said by Yahweh's oracle to be
due to Saul's treatment of the Gibeonites. The watch kept by
Rizpah, Saul's concubine, beneath the dead bodies, two of
which were those of her own children, belongs to this event
(2 Sam. 21). David did not include Meribaal (Mephibosheth),
Jonathan's lame son, in this 'jail-delivery' of the kinsmen of
Saul, but kept him under his eye at the court. There is a
curious mingling of generosity and shrewd policy in more
than one of David's deeds.[1] At the same time, we must not
ignore the great personal qualities which won for him the
devotion and continued loyalty of so many people. He had
the instincts of a leader who can throw himself on the affections of others. He had the right to say 'neither will I offer
burnt offerings unto Yahweh my God which cost me nothing' (24:24). His characteristic impulse when his devoted
men brought him the water of Bethlehem at the peril of their
lives shows us that David's spirit rings true, underneath all
his shrewd policy. He had the great advantage of being free
from outside interference by the Egyptian and Assyrian
Empires. He stands at the beginning of the history of Israel
as an organized and united people, the creator of a great
tradition, even more operative in the realm of religion than
were his actual achievements in making the land one from
Dan unto Beersheba (24:2). He was, as the often misunderstood passage 1 Sam. 13:14 declares, 'a man according
to the purpose of God' (*ish kilebabo*), for he laid the foundations of a great historical development destined to issue in
new and unforeseen ways in David's greater son.

4. Solomon

The accession of Solomon the son of Bathsheba was due,
as we have seen, to the victory of one palace party over
another. Six sons had been born to David during his Hebron

[1] Some scholars (e.g. T. H. Robinson, Benzinger, Stade) regard the
'testament' of David to Solomon, with its legacy of vengeance on Joab
and Shimei, as due to a later attempt to save Solomon's reputation at the
expense of David's. This seems improbable (1 Kings 2:1–12).

period, of whom the four eldest in order were Amnon, Chileab, Absalom, and Adonijah (2 Sam. 3:2ff.). Of these, the son of Abigail, viz., Chileab, is not named elsewhere and doubtless died before any question of the succession arose. Amnon, the natural heir, was killed by Absalom, the next in order, on the ground of the wrong done to Tamar. Absalom himself tried to secure David's place before his death, and himself died. Adonijah, in David's dotage, gathered a strong court party with a view to make the succession his beyond doubt. His supporters included Joab and Abiathar, two of David's right-hand men. But Nathan the prophet, in conjunction with Benaiah the captain of the royal bodyguard and Bathsheba, struck swiftly in order to secure the succession for Bathsheba's son, regardless of primogeniture. With Bathsheba's aid, Nathan was able to mould the helpless and senile king to his purpose, and Solomon was proclaimed king effectively whilst the other party were without military force to back their claims. Adonijah and his two chief supporters were not executed at once, but an opportunity of removing them soon came to Solomon. Adonijah was executed on the ground that his request for Abishag the Shunammite covered designs on the throne, as perhaps it did. Joab was killed by Benaiah whilst clinging to the altar for sanctuary. Abiathar the priest was banished to Anathoth. Another suspect was Shimei the Benjamite; as a kinsman of Saul he had openly cursed David at the time of the rebellion of Absalom, and he might easily become the centre of opposition to Solomon. Accordingly, a pretext for his death was found after some time. On the borders of the kingdom trouble arose for Solomon in the persons of Hadad, an Edomite prince, and Rezon, who established an Aramaean kingdom at Damascus (1 Kings 11). Both of these opponents may be regarded as part of the political legacy taken over by Solomon from David; the opponent who was to prove too much for Solomon's son, viz., Jeroboam, was created by Solomon's own social policy, made necessary by his expenditure on the pleasures of an Oriental ruler. Even the temple was constructed as an adjunct of the palace, as we are told by a later reformer (Ezek. 43:8): Yahweh says through Ezekiel 'there was but the wall between me and them'. Of Solomon's own personality we get no such clear and definite picture as we do of David's. What we do see is the Oriental despot, round whom have gathered a posthumous reputation for wisdom, and a halo of material glory and wealth. The books, ascribed at a much later date to Solomon, viz. Canticles, Ecclesiastes and the 'Wisdom of Solomon', reflect this tradition, and it is not easy to decide just where the historic Solomon ends and the legendary accretions begin. The outstanding facts of history during his reign are the building of the temple, and his systematic administration of the country. The original 'stronghold of Zion', which David captured from the Jebusites and called the 'city of David' (2 Sam. 5:7 ff.), is now usually identified with the southern part of the eastern hill of Jerusalem. Solomon's buildings were erected on the northern part of the same eastern hill. They consisted of the following from the south northwards (1 Kings 6, 7):

1. The House of the Forest of Lebanon (treasure-house and armoury)
2. Hall of Pillars (an assembly-room)
3. Throne-room of Justice
4. Palace
5. Palace of Pharaoh's Daughter
6. Temple

These buildings must have followed the natural disposition of the hill and were therefore partly echeloned towards the west. The altar of burnt-offering in front of the Temple may have been the natural rock, as no account of its construction is given in the list of buildings. If so, it would be the same that projects within the Muhammadan 'Dome of the Rock', now standing on the Temple site.

The scheme of these buildings shows us what an innovation on the simpler days of David was made by Solomon. He was no free-lance like his father, who by personal courage and shrewd policy won the affection and amalgamated the tribal elements of a nation. He reaped where his father had sown, and the reputed size of his harem is a symbol of his 'Orientalism'. His most important alliance was his marriage with Pharaoh's daughter, which brought him the city of Gezer captured by Pharaoh from the Canaanites (who had hitherto held it). Probably this made him the guardian of the great coast road, so important as a channel of trade. With this should be mentioned his alliance for trading and constructive purposes with Hiram, King of Tyre, which was so essential for Solomon's buildings. Israel's art was imported. But with the art and skill and material supplied from without there would come many other elements, which must have done much to raise the scale of civilization in the material sense within Israel. We read of naval expeditions from the Red Sea to Arabia[1] in conjunction with the experienced Phoenicians, and of a great trade in horses with Egypt, and of the building of fortress towns at strategic points which became the nuclei of the increased standing army, including the important addition of cavalry.[2] The economic basis for such developments as these was the levy of forced labour, not confined to surviving Canaanites (as 9:22 declares), but including Israelites (as 5:13 says, in explicit contradiction). The confirmation of this fact is that Jeroboam, from whom the trouble of the next reign was to come, was one of the officials of Solomon, being in charge of the Ephraimite forced labour (1 Kings 11:28). Israel in fact groaned under an Oriental despotism, and was made ready to take the first opportunity to revolt.[3] The whole of the country, with the probable exception of Judah, in whole or in part, had to make contributions to the king's revenue through twelve officers

[1] The phrase 'a navy of Tarshish' (1 Kings 10:22) denotes ships like those which the Phoenicians sent to Tarshish (Tartessus) in Spain.

[2] Excavations at Megiddo have revealed remains of massive installations for housing horses.

[3] The incipient revolt under Jeroboam (1 Kings 11:40) was suppressed, and Jeroboam, who had been urged on by the prophet Ahijah of Shiloh, had to seek refuge in Egypt.

assigned to twelve districts, each district making provision for one month of the year.[1] In this division the older tribal areas were considerably modified; only five of the tribal names appear, and Judah's exemption from this taxation may explain the adhesion of Judah to Rehoboam when Israel broke away.[2] Forced labour was employed in Solomon's building work also, batches of 10,000 labourers being sent for monthly spells in Lebanon. Whether Solomon showed as much wisdom in these sudden economic developments as the Queen of Sheba is reputed to have found in him is open to debate. But we must not lose sight of his important contribution to the history of Israel, i.e., his expansion of the life of the nation, and especially the creation of the Temple at Jerusalem, on a scale which helped to make it ultimately, after some centuries, the one and only sanctuary of Israel.

There were no foreign wars during Solomon's reign, but before the end of it, control of the Aramaeans and of Edom had been lost,[3] to which the policy of a new Pharaoh may have contributed.

[1] David's census (2 Sam. 24) may have been a preliminary to this administrative measure.

[2] See the map in T. H. Robinson's *History of Israel*, p. 264, and note his agreement with Lods, *Israel*, E. T., p. 371.

[3] In 1 Kings 11 : 22, the Lucianic text of the LXX seems original: 'And Hadad returned to his country. This is the evil that Hadad did; and he was oppressive to Israel and reigned over Edom.'

IV.—THE NORTHERN KINGDOM

1. JEROBOAM I

THE separation of Israel from Judah after the death of Solomon was no novel break in old-established relations, but rather a resumption of a previous separation, though with a new cause for embitterment. We have already seen that Judah and Israel settled in Canaan as two distinct groups; their territories were different topographically and therefore in the interests and occupations they afforded; Judah from an early date had absorbed considerable Canaanite and Edomite elements. The union achieved by the popularity and diplomacy of David, and continued by its own momentum under Solomon, had been strained by Solomon's exploitation of Israel for the sake of himself and of Jerusalem. Consequently, it needed little to make Israelite lips cry, 'What portion have we in David?' (1 Kings 12:16). That little was supplied by the initial folly of Solomon's son and successor, Rehoboam, and by the presence of a natural leader of revolt in the person of Jeroboam ben Nebat.

The folly occurred at the national assembly held at the ancient sanctuary-town, Shechem, to confirm the succession of Rehoboam (the significance of such 'election' for the fundamentally democratic character of the kingship should not be overlooked). The complaints against the exactions of the previous reign should have been met by diplomatic concessions, as the older counsellors advised. Instead of this Rehoboam met the complaints with the bluster which usually conceals weakness, and made things worse by sending an unpopular official to deal with the situation. This was

Jeroboam's opportunity. Himself an Ephraimite, and formerly employed by Solomon as superintendent of the forced labour of the Josephite clans, he might have been as unpopular with them as Adoram. But a certain prophet, Ahijah, encouraged him to rebellion (a fact suggesting religious as well as economic unrest) and Jeroboam had to flee from the suspicions of Solomon, and take refuge in Egypt. He now returned, with the halo of the rebel, to foment rebellion, and to become the head of the northern kingdom. Rehoboam's natural but futile desire to appeal to arms was checked by the prophet Shemaiah, in Yahweh's name. Henceforward, until the fall of Samaria in 722, the Hebrew centre of gravity lies in the north, and Judah falls into relative insignificance.

Jeroboam's vigorous instincts as a leader are shown also in his religious policy. To counterbalance the attractive temple of Solomon in Jerusalem, he gave royal support to the two ancient sanctuaries in the extreme north and south of his land, viz., Dan and Bethel. The bull-images of Yahweh which he erected probably represent the continuance of a previous image-cult of Yahweh, derived from the Canaanites, and not belonging to the nomadic period of Israel's religion (for which the Ark may have been the only visible manifestation of His presence). Jeroboam also stabilized the Feast of Tabernacles in the eighth month; in the later Jewish custom (Lev. 23:34), it was held in the seventh. Here again, as in the recognition of non-Levitical priests, Jeroboam appears simply to have continued existent practices, though he is represented by the Deuteronomistic redactor of the Books of Kings as their initiator (1 Kings 12:25–33). He fortified Shechem and made it his capital; Penuel, east of Jordan, also fortified by him, was a second centre.

It was probably owing to the solicitations of Jeroboam that Sheshonk (Shishak) of Egypt invaded the southern kingdom in the fifth year of the reign of Rehoboam. But the Karnak list of conquered cities includes names from the northern kingdom also—Taanach, Megiddo, Penuel, etc.

Possibly Jeroboam had to pay tribute in return for this help, and the names of the tributary cities are included as 'conquests'.

Jeroboam was strong enough to maintain himself as king for twenty-two years, but, after his death, we encounter some of those rapid changes of rule which illustrate the fatal insecurity of tenure characterizing the northern kingdom. His son, Nadab, after a reign of two years, was overthrown by a conspiracy headed by Baasha, who seized his throne. This occurred whilst Nadab was besieging Gibbethon, a fact suggesting the revival of Philistine power. Baasha remained king for twenty-four years, but his son, Elah, after a reign of two years, was overthrown by one of his captains, Zimri, who assassinated him whilst drunk in his palace at Tirzah. Zimri endeavoured, in the oriental way, to make his own position sure by exterminating all the males of Baasha's house, but even this policy of 'Thorough' won him a reign of seven days only. History came near to repeating itself, for Omri, the commander-in-chief of the army again besieging Gibbethon, was made king by his soldiers, and followed up the usurper to the palace at Tirzah. Here Zimri secured remembrance from posterity by firing the palace and dying in its flames.

One incident recorded of Baasha's reign illustrates the significance of Damascus, the centre of Aramaean power, for both Israel and Judah. The state of war initiated by the division of the kingdoms lasted for sixty years, until Jehoshaphat and Ahab formed an alliance. When Baasha of Israel was pressing hard on Asa of Judah, the northern king fortified Ramah, some five miles north of Jerusalem, in order to blockade the capital. Asa in desperation turned to Damascus, and sent to Benhadad such treasure as remained to him to win him as ally against the north. Benhadad promptly responded to the bribe, and descended on Israel, so that Baasha had to abandon his fort. Asa was left free to employ Baasha's building materials in constructing other forts of defence at Geba and Mizpah (15:22).

2. OMRI AND AHAB

Under Omri and the dynasty of three successors which he founded (exceeded only by Jehu's four[1]), the northern kingdom entered on more settled conditions. Omri has been called, from the political standpoint, a northern David, and he was evidently a competent and far-seeing ruler. Like David, he had to face a divided people at the beginning of his reign, since another claimant to the throne, Tibni, maintained himself with a large following for four years. Again, like David, he showed his political sagacity by making a new start with a new capital, when once he had established himself. After six years at Tirzah, he removed to Samaria (16:23). His choice finds ample justification in the fact that it took even such an expert military power as the Assyrians little less than three years to capture it.

Omri's general policy was dictated by the pressure of Damascus. It was of great importance to a trading centre such as Damascus to secure access to the western sea. This largely explains her continued struggles with Israel. Under this pressure, Omri had to give up certain cities to Damascus and also to assign quarters in Samaria itself for Aramaean traders (1 Kings 20:34). The natural counter-weight to Damascus would be Phoenicia. This is the inner meaning of the marriage of Omri's son, Ahab, to Jezebel, the daughter of Ithobal of Tyre (1 Kings 16:31). We get a glimpse of Omri's military successes from the Moabite Stone, which says that 'Omri, king of Israel, afflicted Moab for many days, because Kemosh was angry with his land', and that Israel's supremacy over Moab, won by Omri, lasted all through his reign and half the reign of his son, or more probably, his sons, i.e., forty years in all. A heavy annual tribute was consequently paid by Moab to Israel (2 Kings 3:4).

The importance of Omri is indicated by the fact that Assyrian inscriptions of the following century still designate the northern kingdom as 'the land of Omri'; he has so im-

[1] See Appendix III.

pressed his personality upon it that he has come to be regarded as its true founder.[1] As for his relations with Judah, whilst we have no record of any alliance before the reign of Ahab, there is no reference to any warfare between the two kingdoms, so that Omri may have prepared the way for the definite alliance made by his son. Such alliance, of course, did not mean equality; Judah was always subordinate in power to Israel. But the hostile relations which had prevailed since the division of the kingdom were naturally terminated when Ahab gave his daughter Athaliah in marriage to Joram of Judah (2 Kings 8:18, 25–7), the son of Jehoshaphat. In Ahab's campaign to recover Ramoth-Gilead from Damascus, it was virtually as a vassal king that Jehoshaphat accompanied him (1 Kings 22:1–4).[2] Of course, this would allow for some independence of action, as in Jehoshaphat's naval plans (see p. 75).

The Old Testament tells us more about Ahab than any king since Solomon, a fact which rightly reflects his importance and military activity, however prejudiced its representation of his character. We have also the information supplied by the excavations at Samaria, showing the elaborate buildings of Omri and Ahab, and providing the ostraka which reveal an extensive administrative system.[3] It is not, however, easy to fix the order of military events and to trace the course of the foreign relations with entire confidence. We are told that he was hard pressed by Benhadad, and besieged in Samaria, but that he drove off the Aramaeans by an unexpected sortie (1 Kings 20:1–22). In the campaign of the following year he won a greater victory over Benhadad at Aphek (*vv.* 23–34), the issue of which was a treaty between the two kings, giving the adventage to Israel. Three years after this (22:1) we hear of the attack on Ramoth-

[1] Guthe, *Geschichte*, p. 161.
[2] It is in the story of this campaign that Micaiah appears, a significant figure in the history of the religion. The political activity and influence of the earlier prophets must not be overlooked.
[3] A good account will be found in J. W. Jack's *Samaria in Ahab's Time*.

E

Gilead mentioned above; perhaps this was one of the cities which Benhadad had covenanted to return, without having done so. This was the campaign in which Ahab lost his life by a stray arrow. Prior to it, of course, we must find a place for Ahab's appearance at Karkar (north of Hamath, on the Orontes). Here, according to a cuneiform inscription in the British Museum,[1] Ahab and his army were fighting alongside Benhadad and other Syrian kings, against the Assyrian king Shalmaneser III. The latter, speaking of his campaign against Hamath, says of its king: 'I destroyed, tore down and burned Karkara, his (text: my) royal residence. He brought along to help him 1,200 chariots, 1,200 cavalrymen, 20,000 foot soldiers of Adad-'idri (i.e., Hadadezer [the name given by the Assyrians to Benhadad]) of Damascus, 700 chariots, 700 cavalrymen, 10,000 foot soldiers of Irhuleni from Hamath, 2,000 chariots, 10,000 foot soldiers of Ahab, the Israelite,' etc. No mention of this is made in the O.T. narrative. If it should come before the defeat of Benhadad at Aphek Ahab will be at Karkar as his vassal; if, as seems more likely, between Aphek and Ramoth-Gilead, then Ahab is voluntarily combining with other Syrian states against the Assyrians as a common danger. The battle of Karkar, which seems to have been less decisive than the inscription would suggest, is important from the standpoint of chronology; it gives us the first independently fixed point in the history of Israel and Judah, viz., 853 B.C.

The character of Ahab has been painted for us in dark colours, both by the popular stories about Elijah which have been incorporated into the Books of Kings, and also by the compiler in his summary. His verdict that Ahab 'did that which was evil in the sight of Yahweh above all that were before him' (16:30) is based on the religious consequences of his marriage with Jezebel—the inevitable introduction of the Phoenician Baal into Samaria. Ahab built both a temple and an altar for this foreign Baal, Melkart, in his capital city (16:32). As a religious event, this should be carefully

[1] Pritchard, *A.N.E.T.* p. 278.

distinguished from the steady influence of Canaanite worship in general upon Yahwism, which the prophets of the next century were to attack so vigorously. All the Semitic Baalim were more or less related; they all belonged to the naturalistic type of religion, and therefore stand over against the nomadic moralism of the original worship of Yahweh. But the importation of a foreign cult into the land of Yahweh, and the place given to it in the court through the patronage of the queen, roused the nationalistic spirit as incorporated in Elijah. He rightly felt that the national worship of Yahweh, and His exclusive sovereignty over Israel, were threatened as never before. That is the inner meaning of the Carmel story, and of Elijah's indignant challenge: 'How long are ye limping upon the two different opinions?'[1] We must not think that Ahab had abandoned the worship of Yahweh. The best evidence against that supposition, if evidence were needed, lies in the fact that he gave to each of his three children names which incorporated the name of Yahweh, viz., Ahaziah ('Yahweh has grasped'), Joram or Jehoram ('Yahweh is high') and Athaliah ('Yahweh is great'). But Ahab's recognition of Baal-worship as permissible alongside of Yahweh-worship was not the only point in which he ran counter to the national and prophetic sentiment. The story of Naboth's vineyard and the part it plays in the ultimate overthrow of Omri's dynasty (cf. the words of Jehu, 2 Kings 9:26) supply a good example of what may be called the self-vindicating power of morality. The anti-social act tends to produce a social reaction, so that with inner causality as well as with dramatic fitness, the corpse of Jehoram the son of Ahab will be flung on the ground which his father had so tyrannically seized.

We know nothing of Ahaziah, the son and successor of Ahab, except that he reigned for two years only (1 Kings 22:51–3). He was injured through falling from an upper

---

[1] 'The attempt to combine two religions so incompatible as Yahwe-worship and Ba'al-worship is compared to the laboured gait of a man walking upon legs of different length' (Burney on 1 Kings 18:21).

window of his palace at Samaria; his resort to a Philistine god, Baal-zebub ('Lord of flies')[1] of Ekron, for an oracle as to his recovery, incurred the wrath of Elijah (2 Kings 1:2ff.). His successor was Joram (Jehoram), another son of Ahab, under whom a campaign was undertaken against Moab. Reference has already been made to the Moabite stone, as a first-class contemporary document. The only point in it which raises difficulty in connection with the Biblical record of Joram's campaign is in regard to the date of Mesha's successful rebellion against Israel's supremacy. According to the Stone, Omri had occupied Moabite territory during 'his days (i.e., eighteen years) and half the days of his son (or sons, according as the Moabite consonants are pointed), forty years'. Thus the Stone dates the rebellion either half-way through the reign of Ahab, or half-way through the total reigns of Ahab (22 years), Ahaziah (2) and Joram (12), i.e., in the eighteenth year of Ahab. According to 2 Kings 1:1 and 3:5, the rebellion occurred *after* the death of Ahab, i.e., a few years later. Of the details of Moab's struggle for free-dom, the Old Testament, naturally enough, says nothing. Omri had seized the northern part of the land occupied by Moab, east of the northern half of the Dead Sea, and the Israelites had maintained occupation of this part for forty years. The Moabites were compelled to pay a very large annual tribute of wool, their native product. This mis-fortune, says Mesha (just in the manner of an O.T. writer), was due to the anger of Kemosh against his people. But finally Mesha received the command from his now reconciled god to advance against the enemy. He seized city after city which had been in Israelite occupation, and dedicated the captured vessels of Yahweh to Kemosh, together with thousands of slain Israelites. He built up and fortified the captured cities, and took measures to provide against future sieges by requiring every man to make a water-cistern in his own house. He now dedicates the high place where the Stone

---

[1] This is taken to be a deliberately derogatory form of Baal-zebul 'Baal of the high place'.

originally stood to Kemosh, the author of the deliverance.
The fact that he says of Omri, 'I saw my desire upon him
and his house', may suggest that the Stone was not erected
until after 842, when Jehu had destroyed the dynasty of
Omri. It was to recover possession of the lost territory that
Joram undertook his campaign against Moab, having with
him Jehoshaphat of Judah and an unnamed king of Edom,
through whose territory the expedition made its circuitous
march. It was successful (after difficulties about the water-
supply had been overcome by digging trenches at the
suggestion of Elisha) up to the point of besieging the king
of Moab in Kir-hareseth (Kir of Moab, in the south on
the Wady Kerak). Mesha made a desperate but unavail-
ing attempt to fight his way out; he then sacrificed his
eldest son as a burnt-offering to win the help of the same
god who had given victory before, his national god, Kemosh.
A single obscure verse describes the resultant change in
the situation (a change natural enough psychologically,
if not theologically): 'there came great wrath against
Israel, and they departed from him and returned to
(their) land.' This, of course, means that the invaders were
driven out, and that it was ascribed to the wrath of Kemosh
against Israel aroused by the costly sacrifice (2 Kings
3:27).

Soon after this, Jehoshaphat of Judah was succeeded by
his son Jehoram (8:16ff.), so that there were two kings of
the same name now reigning in the north and in the south.
The Jehoram of the south lost control of Edom (see p. 75);
the Jehoram of the north was also in trouble about this time,
owing to the pressure of the Aramaeans, according to the
narrative of 2 Kings 6:24–7:20—the story of the siege of
Samaria with its gruesome account of mothers driven by
hunger to eat their children, and of the flight of the besiegers
which was discovered by accident through the four lepers.[1]
If a siege of Samaria in the time of Jehoram was brought to

---

[1] The name of the king of Israel who figures in this narrative is not
given; some think that it should be referred to the time of Jehoahaz.

an end in this remarkable manner, the most natural explanation would be the sudden news of some Assyrian attack, recalling the besiegers.

3. THE DYNASTY OF JEHU

The war between Jehoram of Israel and the Aramaeans indirectly led to the remarkable series of events which culminated in the overthrow of the dynasty of Omri. Jehoram was wounded in fighting against the Aramaeans at Ramoth-Gilead (9:14, 15); during his enforced absence at Jezreel, Jehu was in command of the forces of Israel in Ramoth-Gilead. The fuel for a military conspiracy to dethrone Jehoram in favour of Jehu was already there; it was kindled by a messenger from Elisha, and Jehu was proclaimed king on the spot, his temporary throne being fitly enough the soldiers' cloaks flung down upon the steps. The story of the carrying through of the conspiracy forms one of the most dramatic narratives in the Old Testament. Jehu drove his chariot at fullest speed to Jezreel, surprised and killed with his own hand Jehoram, and through his followers also killed Jehoram's nephew, Ahaziah of Judah, who happened to be visiting him.[1] Jehu proceeded to murder Jezebel in the most barbarous fashion, and to procure the murder of seventy relatives of Ahab at Samaria. He is also credited with the murder of forty-two relatives of Ahaziah of Judah, who chanced to fall into his power. In all this baptism of blood, Jehu posed as, and probably believed himself to be, a zealous servant of Yahweh, anointed for his task by Elisha. He was countenanced also by Jehonadab, the founder of the religious tradition belonging to the Rechabites, whose principles were a protest against the Canaanite civilization, as being bound up with the Baal-cult. All the Baal-worshippers were gathered together in the belief that Jehu belonged to their party; he then seized the opportunity to slaughter them all,

[1] The vigour of the Hebrew may be illustrated by 2 Kings 9:27: 'Him also! Pin him to the chariot!' (See L. Waterman, in *The Bible: An American Translation.*)

and thus to show to Jehonadab his zeal for Yahweh.[1] A
century later, men still recalled with horror these bloody
beginnings of a new dynasty; Hosea proclaimed in the name
of Yahweh, 'I will avenge the blood of Jezreel upon the house
of Jehu' (1:4). The compiler of 'Kings' has inserted an
express approval of the very thing which Hosea condemned,
and makes Yahweh say to this blood-stained conspirator,
'thou hast done well' (2 Kings 10:30).

The dynasty of Jehu lasted, however, for a century, i.e., for
half the whole duration of the northern kingdom; it was the
longest dynasty of all in that kingdom of many changes. The
first half of the century (842–c. 800) was marked mainly by
adversity; the second (800–746) by prosperity. The explanation of the change lies in the relation of Israel to the two
external factors affecting her, viz., Damascus and Assyria,
and in their relation to each other. During the reigns of the
first two kings of Jehu's dynasty, viz., Jehu and Jehoahaz,
Damascus dominated Israel; the change came when Damascus
(c. 805) was made tributary to Assyria. During the reign of
Jeroboam II, the most conspicuous figure of this dynasty,
Assyria weakened and lost control of the west. We might,
indeed, almost generalize and say that Israel and Judah
were never politically strong unless their neighbours were
weak or engrossed in their own affairs.

Damascus had become the important centre she was
because of the natural fertility of her soil, created by the
river Abana (Barada) flowing from the Lebanons. This made
her the frontier city of Syria facing east, and the centre of
great roads, west and south and east, on which Arab caravans
would naturally converge.[2] She must be to-day one of the
oldest surviving cities of the world, though her first recorded
appearance in history is only in the lists of Egyptian conquests of the sixteenth century B.C., and in the Amarna

[1] Even so keen a Yahwist as Jehu does not seem to have regarded the
bull-images as derogatory to Yahweh.
[2] A glance at a good map of the Semitic world will show this; cf.
G. A. Smith, *Historical Geography of the Holy Land*, last chapter, and the
map of 'Ancient Trade Routes' on p. 6 of his 'Atlas'.

records of the fifteenth. David (2 Sam. 8:5ff.) had come into
conflict with the Aramaeans who centred in Damascus, but
Damascus was never part of the territory of Israel. Asa of
Judah (1 Kings 15:18) had appealed to Benhadad of Damascus for help against Baasha of Israel, and had obtained it;
Benhadad had compelled Omri of Israel to give him trading
rights in Samaria. Benhadad II was defeated by Ahab, and
that relation reversed. At the battle of Karkar in 853, we
saw that Israel fought by the side of Damascus and other
Syrian states against the Assyrians under Shalmaneser III.
This brings us to the period with which we are now concerned, for Hazael, the assassin and successor of Benhadad II,
was the contemporary of Jehu.

Assyria first came into effective contact with the Syrian
states of Israel's times through the revival of Assyrian power
under Ashurnazirpal II (884–859). In 868 he invaded
northern Palestine and penetrated into Phoenicia, though
without touching Damascus and Israel. The first contact
with them was made through his son, Shalmaneser III, at the
battle of Karkar in 853; but his victory was not followed up,
perhaps owing to difficulties in other parts of the Assyrian
empire, until the year of Jehu's revolt. In the more remote
centuries of Mesopotamian history Assyria had been relatively small and subordinated to the Sumerians and to the
Babylonians in the south. She came to the front in the
thirteenth and twelfth centuries, but again became relatively
unimportant until the times of Ashurnazirpal II in the ninth
century. From the days of his son until the fall of Nineveh
in 612, the fortunes of Israel and Judah continued to be
more or less affected by Assyria, though Damascus was an
important intervening factor—a buffer state—until her overthrow by the Assyrians in 732.[1]

Against such a background, therefore, we must conceive
the history of the century of Jehu's dynasty. Throughout it,
Judah is but the thistle where Israel is the cedar (2 Kings
14:9), as the fate of Amaziah when unduly elated by his

[1] See Appendix IV, The Imperial Backgrounds.

victory over Edom sufficiently shows (*vv.* 12 ff.). In the first
year of Jehu's reign, Shalmaneser conducted a successful
campaign against some of the Syrian states, including
Damascus, which put large forces into the field. Shalmaneser
marched to the Mediterranean coast and received tribute
from the Tyrians, the Sidonians and from Jehu himself. On
the 'Black Obelisk' of the British Museum we can see Jehu
prostrating himself before the Assyrian king, whilst beneath
it is a schedule of the tribute paid.[1] The fierce attack made
upon Israel by Hazael of Damascus soon afterwards was
probably due to the fact that Jehu had withdrawn from the
usual Syrian coalition and secured his own safety from
Assyria by paying tribute. In thus attacking Israel under
Jehu, Hazael was departing from the rôle ascribed to him by
Yahweh through Elijah (1 Kings 19:15 ff.) and Elisha
(2 Kings 8:13), which was to chastise the house of Ahab;
in fact Elisha had practically instigated Hazael to assassinate
Benhadad, though he is represented as foreseeing that
Hazael would be guilty of atrocious deeds against Israel.
As a result of Hazael's attack, Israel lost about a third of her
territory, i.e., that on the east of the Jordan (10:32–4). This
is what Amos had in mind a couple of generations later when
he said that the Aramaeans 'have threshed Gilead with
threshing-instruments of iron' (1:3). This tyrannical and
cruel oppression of Israel by the unforgiving Aramaeans
continued through more than one reign. Jehu, after reigning
for twenty-eight years, was succeeded by his son Jehoahaz
(815–801) of whose time it is said that 'the anger of Yahweh
was kindled against Israel and He delivered them into the
hand of Hazael, king of Syria, and into the hand of Benhadad, the son of Hazael, continually' (2 Kings 13:3). This
has been described as the period of Israel's greatest humiliation; the military strength of Israel was reduced to its lowest
point by a 'limitation of armaments'; the king of Syria 'left
not to Jehoahaz of the people save fifty horsemen and ten

---

[1] J. B. Pritchard, *The Ancient Near East in Pictures*, 1954 [*A.N.E.P.*]
1–5; for text see *A.N.E.T.* p. 281.

chariots and ten thousand footmen: for the king of Syria destroyed them and made them like the dust to trample on' (13:7). Hazael's mastery over Israel is shown by the fact that he could penetrate as far south as the Philistine city of Gath, which he captured (12:17), and that Jehoash of Judah had to buy him off from capturing Jerusalem by the sacrifice of all the treasures of the temple and of the palace (v. 18). Also, after Elisha's death, we hear of the Moabites making it a yearly practice to invade Israel (13:20), a sure sign of the weakness to which both the kingdoms were now reduced before the might of Damascus. Relief was not obtained until the reign of Jehoash of Israel (801–786), the grandson of Jehu, who recovered the lost cities in three victories.[1] Doubtless this recovery of Israel was due to renewed Assyrian pressure on Damascus. We know that Rammannirari (Adadnirari III, 810–783) was exacting tribute from Syrian states in the years 806–3, whilst special emphasis is laid on his victory over Damascus in 803.[2]

The most important and successful king of Jehu's dynasty was Jeroboam II (786–746), under whom the prophets Amos and Hosea initiated a new epoch in the history of the religion of Israel. Jeroboam II seems to be the 'saviour' indicated in 2 Kings 13:5 (cf. 2 Kings 14:27: 'Yahweh saved them by the hand of Jeroboam'), who completed the deliverance begun under Jehoash. Little is told us—far too little for his evident importance—in the direct narrative, except that 'he restored the border of Israel from the entering in of Hamath unto the sea of the Arabah, according to the word of Yahweh, the God of Israel, which he spake by the hand of his servant Jonah the son of Amittai, the prophet, which was of Gath-hepher'—a prophet of whom nothing else is known (14:25). This extract from the ancient annals shows an extension of the kingdoms of Judah and Israel, of course under Israel's supremacy, to the limits of the old Davidic kingdom, except

[1] 13:25; note the significance of the 'prophetic symbolism' of vv. 14–19.
[2] The Calah inscription in Pritchard, *A.N.E.T.* p. 281.

possibly some territory in the north-east districts. Our real knowledge of this reign, however, is gained from the contemporary prophecies of Amos and Hosea, and it is incomparably greater and more secure, especially in regard to the social and religious conditions, than for any period since that of David and Solomon. From their prophecies we can see that this was a time of sudden and unexampled prosperity, with all its social and religious perils, that the religion was outwardly flourishing, but in quality decadent, and that the inevitable fate of the various Syrian kingdoms was to be swallowed up into the might of Assyria. The temporary prosperity was due to the preoccupation of Damascus with the Assyrians, and of the Assyrians with internal difficulties.

Zechariah, the last representative of the dynasty of Jehu, reigned for six months only, and was assassinated by a usurper, Shallum. Thus the dynasty ended, as it had begun, in bloodshed, justifying the word of Amos, 'I will rise against the house of Jeroboam with the sword' (7:9; cf. 2 Kings 15:10).

4. The Decline and Fall of Israel

The period immediately before us is only one quarter the length of the last; instead of the century of Jehu's dynasty we have the quarter of a century from the fifth and last descendant of Jehu to the fall of Samaria in 722. But time is measured by events rather than events by time; the events of this quarter of a century move swiftly as a river in its rapids. The external factors were as before Damascus and Assyria—Damascus by her alliance with Israel against Judah and Assyria, Assyria by her revival of interest in the west under Tiglath-Pileser III. As for the northern kingdom of Israel, her position at the beginning of this period is aptly portrayed by the contemporary prophet Hosea (7:8–11):

Ephraim, he mixeth himself among the peoples;
Ephraim is a cake not turned.
Strangers have devoured his strength and he knoweth it not;

Yea, grey hairs are sprinkled upon him and he knoweth it
    not.
. . . Ephraim is like a silly dove, without understanding;
They call unto Egypt, they go to Assyria.

The reference in the last line is to the alternative policies
of the politicians of the day; they would be either pro-
Assyrian or pro-Egyptian, since a relatively small Syrian
state like Ephraim must ultimately depend on one or the
other of the great empires which were her neighbours.

In some respects we might compare the change from the
apparent prosperity of the reign of Jeroboam in Israel with
that in the south from the conditions under Solomon to those
of his successor, Rehoboam, except that the consequences in
the north were much more serious and soon beyond remedy.
Between the flourishing reign of Jeroboam II, who raised
Israel to such a height of prosperity (786–746), and the fall of
Samaria (722), implying the overthrow of Israel, there is the
collapse of a civilization. The judgment of the two great
contemporary prophets, viz., Amos and Hosea, shows that
they rightly discerned the frailty of the prosperity in the first
half of the century. Amos at the royal sanctuary of Bethel
declares, in connection with his vision of Yahweh measuring
a wall with a plumbline (7:7ff.) 'the high places of Isaac shall
be desolate, and the sanctuaries of Israel shall be laid waste:
and I will rise against the house of Jeroboam with the
sword'. Hosea is divinely ordered to call Gomer's son by the
symbolic name 'Jezreel', in allusion to the event told in
2 Kings 10:11: 'Jehu smote all that remained of the house
of Ahab in Jezreel'; and the reason given to the prophet is
'yet a little while, and I will avenge the blood of Jezreel
upon the house of Jehu' (Hos. 1:4). The fulfilment of this
moral judgment and political vision is partly seen in the
rapid succession of kings in the northern kingdom—no less
than six come and go in the score of years between the death
of Jeroboam and the final siege of Samaria. Hosea's later
prophecies reflect this feature: cf. 8:4, 'they have set up

kings, but not by me; they have made princes and I knew it not'; 10:3, 'Surely now shall they say, We have no king: for we fear not Yahweh, and the king, what can he do for us?'; 13:10, 11, 'Where is now thy king, that he may save thee in all thy cities? and thy judges, of whom thou saidst, Give me a king and princes? I have given thee a king in mine anger, and have taken him away in my wrath.' Political anarchy combined with social corruption to bring the northern kingdom to its appointed end.

The first of these brief reigns is that of Zechariah the son of Jeroboam, who succeeded his father in 746 and reigned for six months (2 Kings 15:8–12). All we know is that he was killed in a conspiracy headed by Shallum.[1] The usurper Shallum did not maintain his position for more than a month (15:13–16); he was slain by Menahem, who had made Tirzah, once the capital of the kingdom (1 Kings 14:17; 15:21; 16:6), his centre of operations. The cruelty of Menahem after his reduction of a town held by the rival party is specially signalized (2 Kings 15:16). Menahem (745–737: not 'ten years' as in 15:17) retained sovereignty for a few years, towards the close of which the shadow cast by Assyria significantly deepened. In the Biblical annals we read (15:19, 20): 'There came against the land Pul the king of Assyria; and Menahem gave Pul a thousand talents of silver, that his hand might be with him to confirm the kingdom in his hand. And Menahem exacted the money of Israel, even of all the mighty men of wealth, of each man fifty shekels of silver, to give to the king of Assyria. So the king of Assyria turned back, and stayed not there in the land.' In the Assyrian annals of 738, the name of Menahem of Samaria appears in a considerable list of other tributaries,[2] though no separate details are given. The king is Tiglath-Pileser III, and Samaria was one of nineteen Syrian states which united against Assyria. This is the first time that Assyria is seen to intervene in the inner affairs of Israel; Menahem received

[1] 15:10; for the prophecy of v. 12, see 10:30.
[2] Pritchard, A.N.E.T. p. 283.

Assyrian support in return for the tribute he paid. The talent is taken at about 3,000 shekels, so that a tribute of a thousand talents at fifty shekels a head shows that there were 60,000 people to be assessed in Israel (this may include Judah). So far as we know, Menahem died a natural death, and was succeeded by his son Pekahiah, who was not so fortunate. Within two years, Pekahiah was killed in his citadel at Samaria by his adjutant, Pekah, and a band of fifty Gileadites. The fact that they come from Eastern Palestine suggests the co-operation of Damascus in the deed; at all events Pekah came to represent what we may call the Aramaizing, as distinct from the Assyrian, party. Both Menahem and his son Pekahiah had accepted vassaldom to Assyria; Pekah, on the other hand, formed an alliance with Damascus and other Syrian states against Assyria (the opportunity being given by Assyria's preoccupation with Urartu). Previous to this alliance, from which sprang the Syro-Ephraimitic war with Judah, we may date the prophecy of Isaiah, which proclaims 'The Doom of Ephraim' (9:8–10:4; 5:25–30). This declares that Ephraim's pride is to be humbled by enemies on both sides of her, and that her attempts to recover from the losses of the previous years—such, we may suppose, as Menahem's tribute to Assyria, and the anarchy of the whole decade since 743—are doomed to failure:

Proudly and greatly daring (they said)
'Bricks have fallen, but with hewn stone we will rebuild;
Sycamores have been cut down, but with cedars will we
    replace them.'[1]

Isaiah foresees a day of overwhelming disaster, marked by civil war, Manasseh against Ephraim. He singles out the social injustices of the time, the wrongs done by unjust judges, as the particular cause of Yahweh's approaching judgment. The final destruction of Ephraim will come from a resistless foe, evidently intended to be the Assyrians. How-

[1] G. B. Gray's version, *Isaiah*, p. 177.

ever, before this prophecy found even partial fulfilment in the Assyrian invasion of 733, Isaiah was to be concerned with the fortunes of Judah under the menace of attack from Ephraim and Damascus,[1] of which more will be said in the account of the southern kingdom (p. 78 f.). Ahaz refused to share the confidence of Isaiah that this menace would have no result, and secured the aid of Assyria, which invaded the eastern territory of the northern kingdom. We read in 2 Kings 15:29 that 'In the days of Pekah king of Israel came Tiglath-Pileser, king of Assyria, and took Ijon and Abel-beth-Maacah and Janoah and Kedesh and Hazor and Gilead and Galilee, all the land of Naphtali, and he carried them captive to Assyria.' This conquest of territory meant that the northern kingdom was now confined to the hill-country of Ephraim and the plain of Esdraelon; the rest was made into an Assyrian province.[2] Pekah suffered the fate of unsuccessful kings and was killed by Hoshea, a pro-Assyrian. Hoshea was installed in his place by the Assyrians, and the diminished kingdom slipped back into the position of five years previously, when Menahem paid tribute to Assyria. Damascus, reduced after a siege which extended into two years, suffered a worse fate; its people were deported and Rezin was executed. Thus ended the history of the Aramaeans in Damascus, after the two centuries in which they had so often and so closely been concerned in the history of Israel. It was to be another decade before Samaria suffered the same fate.

Both the depopulation of Galilee and the overthrow of Damascus are described on the Assyrian monuments. Of the former, we read:

Bit Khumria

... the entirety of its people
their goods to Assyria I carried away. As Pekah, their king,
they had deposed, Hosea

[1] Isaiah 17:1–11, 'The Coming Destruction of Syria and Ephraim' seems to follow the above, as it presupposes the alliance, but to precede 7, 8, i.e., it dates c. 733 B.C.

[2] See map in T. H. Robinson's *History of Israel*, p. 381.

I established as king over them. Ten talents of gold . . .
. . . talents of silver I received as present from them.[1]

(According to 2 Kings 15:30, Hoshea killed his predecessor.)
In the decade between the overthrow of Damascus and the
capture of Samaria we get a contemporary glimpse of the
northern kingdom through the eyes of prophets of the south.
Isaiah 28:1–4 deals with 'the drunkards of Ephraim', whom
he pictures as flower-crowned revellers at a banquet, with a
secondary reference in the manner of Oriental poetry to the
position of Samaria itself, as a city crowning a hill:

> Ha! proud crown of the drunkards of Ephraim,
> And fading flower of his beauty of adornment,
> On the heads of the wine-smitten!
> Behold, the Lord hath a mighty one and a strong,
> Like a downpour of hail, like a storm of destruction,
> Like a downpour of mighty waters overflowing,
> Will he level to the earth in might.
> The proud crown of the drunkards of Ephraim
> Shall be trampled with the feet,
> The fading flower of his beauty of adornment
> On the head of the fertile valley
> Shall be as the first-ripe fig ere the fruit-gathering,
> Which as soon as a man sees, and it is in his hand,
> He swallows it.

Similarly, in plainer language, Micah (1:5, 7) says:

> What is the transgression of Jacob? is it not Samaria? . . .
> Therefore will I make Samaria as an heap of the field, and
> as the plantings of a vineyard: and I will pour down the
> stones thereof into the valley, and I will lay bare the
> foundations thereof.

The Assyrian puppet-king Hoshea retained his nominal
position from 732 to 724. The account of his fall, and with
it that of the northern kingdom, is brief, though the Deutero-

[1] Pritchard, *A.N.E.T.* p. 284.

nomistic compiler expatiates on its moral at length (2 Kings 17:3–6). The order of events is, first, the defection of Hoshea, through a plan of rebellion encouraged by Sabe or Sibi (not Sabako), a leading general of Egypt, in 724; then the imprisonment of Hoshea, then the siege of Samaria for nearly three years, closing successfully in 722, then the deportation of inhabitants, who, as we learn from *vv.* 24 ff., were replaced by settlers from other subject lands. The king under whom the earlier part of these things occurred was Shalmaneser V (726–722); Samaria fell immediately after his death so that his successor Sargon II was able to claim the victory. The Assyrian records are[1]:

> In the beginning of my reign (722) and in the first year of my reign (721) . . . Samaria I besieged and took . . . 27,290 inhabitants I carried away, 50 chariots I collected there as a royal force . . . I set up again and made more populous than before. People from lands which I had taken I settled there. My men I set over them as governors. Tribute and taxes like the Assyrian I set over them.

Thus ended the history of the northern kingdom, Israel, as thus began the history of those 'Samaritans', who figure so largely in later Jewish history. The actual colonization of Samaria was not accomplished at one stroke; the inscriptions give more than one reference to settlements. There was a further, but ineffective, revolt in which 'Samaritans' took part in 720.

[1] Pritchard, *A.N.E.T.* p. 284.

F

V.—THE SOUTHERN KINGDOM

As we turn from the northern to the southern kingdom, we cannot but be impressed by certain striking contrasts in the characters of the two histories. Most obvious of all is that of duration and stability. The northern kingdom lasted for little more than a couple of centuries, and included eight revolutionary changes of dynasty or ruler. The southern kingdom lasted for nearly three and a half centuries after the withdrawal of Israel, or for more than four centuries when we include the reigns of David and Solomon, and all this time under a single dynasty of Davidic descent. How shall we explain this remarkable difference? First, no doubt, by the difference of position. The southern kingdom lay off the high road between east and west, and Jerusalem was a very difficult place to carry by assault, whereas the northern kingdom was much more open to invasion, and its control was essential to Aramaea or Assyria if the Mediterranean coast was to be open to them. Then we must reckon the greater military resources of the north as themselves perilous to internal continuity. Baasha, Zimri, Omri, Jehu, Shallum, Pekah and Hoshea all seized the throne by a military *coup d'état*; the most notable parallel in the south was the *restoration* by armed force of a Davidic prince in place of the queen-mother, Athaliah. A third important difference is in the relation of politics and religion. In the north, religion tended to be a phase of politics, as witness the religious policy of Jeroboam, Omri and Ahab, Jehu; in the south, we shall see religion breaking away from and rising above politics, in the personal faith of Isaiah and Jeremiah, and in the religious reformations of (possibly) Hezekiah and (certainly) Josiah. Religion can never be a substitute for politics, but the recognition of higher values than those of mere expediency will always in the long run make for stability in politics. A fourth difference, as we shall see, relates to the way in which the two kingdoms were treated finally by their conquerors, though this also is bound up with their different degrees of religious development. Those deported by Assyria were scattered and lost to history, whilst foreign colonists in Samaria helped to change its character into that of an Assyrian province. Those deported from Judaea by the Babylonians were allowed to maintain their national unity, and to develop the inheritance of their faith and literature, with consequences of the utmost importance to the whole world.

The first period in the history of the southern kingdom is terminated by the revolution of Jehu in 842, which affected, though temporarily, the south as well as the north. This period is dominated by the superior position of the northern kingdom and is characterized by the general relation of the southern kingdom to it, one of hostility followed by one of alliance. The second period, presenting a marked contrast of adversity followed by prosperity in the southern kingdom, may conveniently extend to the death of Azariah (Uzziah) in 742. The third may be called, even in such a general history as this, the age of Isaiah. The fourth is concerned with the interplay of politics and religion in the seventh century. The fifth covers the Babylonian period from Carchemish (605) to the end of the state in 586.

1. HOSTILITY AND ALLIANCE

The circumstances which led to the withdrawal of Israel from Judah have been sufficiently indicated in the previous chapter, but something more must be said of its sequel, the invasion of Judah by Sheshonk of Egypt, in the fifth year of Rehoboam. The treasures of the temple and of the palace were plundered, including the famous shields of gold made by Solomon (1 Kings 10:17). Rehoboam was reduced to imitation-shields of bronze for his processional displays. In the Karnak inscription,[1] showing chained captives, each bearing the name of a conquered city, there are about a hundred names of Judaean towns. This invasion and loss of treasure must have been a heavy blow to the southern kingdom, and one given at a time when it had already fallen into a position of inferiority to its northern neighbour. We know nothing else of Rehoboam's reign (922–915), except that 'there was war continually between him and Jeroboam' (14:30). After a reign of seven years, he was succeeded by his son Abijam or Abijah, who reigned three years, to be succeeded by his son (or brother) Asa, who reigned for forty-one years (912–872). The compiler praises him for his partial reformation of religion, including the removal of certain sexual developments of the cult which had come in from Canaanite sources, and had been patronized by his grandfather (or father) Rehoboam, on the initiative of his wife (Rehoboam's mother had been Ammonite).[2] It is a curious example of the flotsam and jetsam of historical remembrance which floats down the stream of time, that we should be told of him, 'in the time of his old age he was diseased in his feet'.[3] Reference has already been made to the attack upon Asa by Baasha of Israel (p. 53), frustrated by the intervention of Damascus.

Under the next king of Judah, viz., Jehoshaphat (872–849), we find a change in the relations of the two kingdoms

---

[1] *E.Bi.*, 1243, 4, where part of the representation is reproduced. Cf. Gressmann, *ABAT*[2], Tafel 1, fig. 114; also Pritchard, *A.N.E.P.* No. 349.

[2] Cf. Sellin, *Geschichte des isr.-jüd. Volkes*, I, p. 205. Note that 1 Kings 15:8, makes Asa the son of Abijah, whilst *v.* 10 implies that they were brothers.

[3] The Book of Chronicles adds to this by saying, 'in his disease he sought not to Yahweh, but to the physicians' (2 Chron. 16:12), to show that he was guilty of the same want of faith as when he resorted to Damascus to save him from Israel. The Chronicler ascribes to Asa a remarkable victory over an Ethiopian army of a million men (2 Chron. 14:9), whilst of his father (or brother) Abijah, it is told that he defeated Jeroboam and slew half a million Israelites (13:17). These statements show how difficult it is to make any use of the Chronicler for the early history.

and hostility passes into alliance, in the sense that Judah becomes virtually the vassal of Israel. It is in this light that Jehoshaphat appears in Ahab's campaign against Ramoth-Gilead (see p. 55). Further, Ahab gave Athaliah, his daughter, in marriage to Jehoram, the son and future successor of Jehoshaphat, a marriage destined to have grave consequences in the south. Jehoshaphat was also concerned in the campaign of Jehoram, the son of Ahab, against Moab (see p. 59) which ended unsuccessfully. A third partner in this campaign was an unnamed king of Edom (2 Kings 3:9). At this time, Edom was apparently in a vassal relation to Judah. Jehoshaphat used the opportunity given by this control of Edom to build a large ship[1] to sail from Ezion-geber (on the eastern arm of the Red Sea, the Gulf of Akabah) to Ophir, perhaps on the Arabian shore of the Persian Gulf. The ship was wrecked at the outset of her voyage, but Jehoshaphat refused the proferred partnership of Ahaziah the son of Ahab in the enterprise (1 Kings 22:47-9). This suggests that relative independence of action remained to Judah, as of course the 'vassal' relation would allow. The control of Edom by Judah was, however, temporary.[2] In the time of Jehoshaphat's son and successor, Jehoram (849-842), Edom successfully revolted; the Judaean king was so hard pressed when he tried to overcome the revolt that he and his captains had to fight their way out by night through the ranks of the surrounding Edomites (2 Kings 8:21). (Libnah, a Philistine city, is said to have revolted at the same time.) The next king of Judah, viz., Ahaziah, who succeeded his father Jehoram at the age of twenty-two, had but a single year's reign, for he was swept into the orbit of Jehu's lust for blood. Ahaziah had accompanied his uncle Jehoram of Israel in a campaign against Ramoth-gilead, just as his grandfather,

---

[1] The text is uncertain; it may have meant one ship or it may have meant a fleet.

[2] The changing relations between Judah and Edom may be instructively compared with those between Israel and Damascus, though Edom, of course, never attained to the historical importance of Damascus.

Jehoshaphat, had accompanied Ahab in a similar campaign. When Jehoram was wounded and had returned from the front to Jezreel, Ahaziah visited him, and was there when Jehu arrived, to slay both uncle and nephew (see p. 60).

2. ADVERSITY AND PROSPERITY

Jehu's actions in the north had a curious echo in the south, where the throne was seized by the 'queen-mother' Athaliah (mother of the slain Ahaziah and the last survivor of the house of Ahab). To ensure her tenure she followed Jehu's example in killing all who could challenge her position, which meant all her own male relatives. Her year-old grandchild, Jehoash, the son of Ahaziah, alone escaped her notice, because he was hidden by his aunt, Jehosheba, who was, according to the Chronicler (2 Chron. 22:11), the wife of Jehoiada the priest. The Davidic dynasty depended on a slender thread whilst the infant Jehoash was in hiding in the temple. When he was seven years old, however, Jehoiada contrived a successful plot to overthrow Athaliah. He secured the support of the royal guard (who were foreigners, as in the time of David) and concentrated them all in the temple, when its regular guard was being changed. Here Jehoash was crowned king, and Athaliah arrived on the scene only to be assassinated. A religious motive mingled with the political, for the temple of Baal was overthrown and its priest slain. Thus the rising in the south against the last representative of the dynasty of Omri shared in the religious motive of the rebellion of Jehu; the difference was that the prophets Elijah and Elisha were replaced by the priest Jehoiada. That may well indicate a different quality in the established religion of the two kingdoms.

Jehoash (837–800) reigned nearly forty years, but the only incidents of that period which are recorded are the measures he took to ensure the proper repair of the temple (still a royal chapel) and his enforced surrender of treasure to Hazael of Damascus, who at this time had both Israel and Judah at his mercy (see p. 64). One or other of these actions[1] may have led to the conspiracy against him which resulted in his assassination (2 Kings 12:21). His action in regard to the temple seems to have been to transfer the cost of repairs from the royal exchequer to the temple dues and voluntary offerings of the people.[2] The expenditure was left to the priests, but this proved unsatisfactory, as the repairs were neglected, so the task was transferred to lay control, which ensured a proper expenditure (2 Kings 12:4–16). This measure was taken in the twenty-third year of Jehoash, so that its effect, if any, in making him unpopular with the priesthood, had no immediate result. In this connection might be named an incident recorded by the Chronicler (2 Chron. 24:17 ff.) as taking place after the death of Jehoiada the priest, viz., a revival of the Baal cult fostered by the nobility and the king; this led to the execution of Jehoiada's son, the priest Zechariah, who protested against it. The Chronicler characteristically connects this with the second event, viz., the invasion of Judah by Hazael, which is regarded as the divine penalty for the paganism. The humiliation of the surrender to Hazael (2 Kings 12:17, 18) would certainly tend to make Jehoash unpopular with the people, whilst the alienation of the priesthood may have been a secondary factor in the events leading to his assassination.

Amaziah (800–783), his son and successor, executed the assassins, but not their children, a fact thought worthy of record as an innovation on the older conception of corporate personality. A striking victory over the Edomites encouraged him to the folly of challenging Jehoash of Israel, with dire results (2 Kings 14:7 ff.). Amaziah's troops were routed, part of the wall of Jerusalem was broken down to make it defenceless, and treasure and hostages were taken. This has been described as the greatest humiliation of the house of David.[3]

---

[1] Jirku, *Geschichte des Volkes Israel*, p. 187, takes the former view; Sellin, *op. cit.*, p. 229, the latter.

[2] So Skinner, *Kings*, p. 342.

[3] Dennefeld, *Histoire d'Israël*, p. 126.

We do not know any details of the recovery from this
political nadir, which must have taken place in the long
reign of Azariah (Uzziah) (783–742). Of this king himself we
know nothing, except that he became a leper and that his son
Jotham acted as regent. It is clear, however, that prosperity
had been fully regained before the age of Isaiah. This
prosperity of the south is parallel with that of the north
under Jeroboam II; its most natural explanation is that after
the turn of the century Damascus had been weakened, and
that Assyria was not yet concerned with other Syrian states,
e.g., Judah. They were therefore free to develop, especially
in trading. The Chronicler, in fact, records that Azariah
recovered Elath (the port on the Gulf of Akabah) from the
Edomites, and fortified it (2 Chron. 26:2). There seems to be
no sufficient ground for identifying Azariah with Azariah of
Ja'udi mentioned in the annals of Tiglath-Pileser.[1]

3. The Age of Isaiah

Isaiah dates his call (6) by a reference to the death of
Uzziah (Azariah), the last named king, i.e., in 742,[2] and
editorial notes tell us that his prophecies extend over the
next three reigns (1:1). For this period, therefore, we have
the advantage of evidence that is contemporary. Early in
the period, he is a prominent figure in the reaction of Judah
to the 'Syro-Ephraimitic' menace; towards its end, he is
equally prominent in the events connected with Sennacherib's invasion of Judah. On these events and on others
lying between them, his comments are of great historical
importance.

Our sources of knowledge of the Syro-Ephraimitic War
are three, viz., Isaiah 7:1–8:18, 2 Kings 15, 16, and the two
inscriptions of Tiglath-Pileser.[3] It is clear that the object in
attacking Judah was to compel her to fall into line with

[1] See Pritchard A.N.E.T. p. 282. O. Procksh in his commentary on
Isaiah 1–39, p. 2, accepts the identification.
[2] The entrance of Tiglath-Pileser III about this time into the World of
Syrian politics may have been the external occasion of Isaiah's 'call'.
[3] Pritchard, A.N.E.T. pp. 282–4.

other Syrian states against Assyria. Pressure began in the reign of Jotham (742–735), but the threatened siege of Jerusalem by the allies falls in the reign of his son, the youthful Ahaz (735–715). Isaiah's memoirs have preserved a striking scene in which both he and the king figure. At a moment when panic, like a wind in the trees of the forest, has swept over the city, and Ahaz is inspecting the defences, Isaiah meets him 'by the channel of the upper pool', and speaks scornfully of the enemies' attempt to replace him by a puppet king who will play their game. The two hostile kings are no more than smouldering firebrands—'smoke not fire' (Gray); let him have faith in the purpose of Yahweh to protect His city against them. 'If you will not trust firmly, you will not be confirmed'—so we may render the paronomasia of Isaiah's great saying about faith which marks a theological epoch as the first historical demand for it.[1] Such a saying recalls the remark of Kittel concerning Isaiah: 'His thoughts have become history.' Ahaz, however, refused to respond, even when the prophet offered to confirm his message with a divine sign. Instead, Ahaz appealed to Tiglath-Pileser, with appropriate gifts, to deliver him from his danger, which the Assyrian king promptly did.

After the Syro-Ephraimitic War of 734, Judah under Ahaz was a tributary state to Assyria, though not an Assyrian province. As a result of the Assyrian campaigns of that time, new Assyrian provinces had been created in Palestine, and when Samaria itself became one of these in 722, few tributary states were left—the Philistine and Phoenician coast-lands, with Ammon, Moab and Edom—besides Judah.[2] The organization of the neighbouring Samaria as an Assyrian province brought Assyria for the first time into actual contact with Judah, but occasioned no further change; the submissive policy of Ahaz was (at first) continued by Hezekiah (715–687), his successor; the Assyrian policy was to leave in

---

[1] The only passage possibly earlier is Gen. 15:6: 'Abram had faith in Yahweh, and He reckoned it to him for righteousness.'

[2] See the map in T. H. Robinson's *History of Israel*, p. 381.

peace the tributary states on the borders of its provinces.
Soon after the fall of Samaria, there was a renewal of revolt
in Palestine[1] in which Hamath in the north-east, Gaza, and
some of the newly-formed provinces took part, including
Samaria, or at least some of its people, with Egyptian aid.
In 720 Sargon suppressed this rebellion, in which Judah had
no share. (No prophecies of Isaiah relate to it.) We hear of
no further revolt in Palestine for a decade, but in 711, the
Assyrian inscriptions[2] tell us of a campaign of Sargon against
Ashdod in the course of which Judah took part, together
with Edom and Moab and the Philistines, and again with
aid from Egypt. The result was that the district of Ashdod
was re-settled with people deported from the East, and
constituted a new Assyrian province. The Old Testament
does not directly mention Judah's participation in this revolt,
but we have an oracle of Isaiah that refers to it (20), the
oracle which was given by deed as well as word, through
Isaiah going about in the garb of a captive to represent the
ultimate fate of Egypt, on which the coalition as usual relied.

Isaiah's opposition to the pro-Egyptian policy was consistent; as we shall see in reviewing his important influence
on public policy, he was opposed to all diplomacy and all
alliances, and advocated a purely religious mission for Israel,
in reliance on the sure protection of Yahweh, whilst politically
she remained under Assyrian rule, till Yahweh's Kingdom
came. This attitude is tersely illustrated in 14:32:

> What then shall one answer the messengers of the
> nation? That Yahweh hath founded Zion, and in her shall
> the afflicted of His people take refuge.

This attitude is again illustrated in connection with the
embassy of Merodach-baladan, the usurper of the kingdom of
Babylon, who gave so much trouble to its Assyrian overlords.
The embassy was ostensibly despatched to congratulate
Hezekiah on his recovery from sickness (2 Kings 20:12ff.),

---

[1] Pritchard, *A.N.E.T.* p. 285.
[2] Id. p. 286.

but there can be no doubt that it covered some one of the numerous conspiracies against the Assyrian empire of which these years are so full. Hezekiah is represented as displaying his resources to the embassy, whereupon Isaiah prophesied their ultimate capture. We cannot be certain as to the date of this particular event, since the whole chronology of Hezekiah's reign is matter of dispute; but the period shortly before the Ashdod revolt would suit it best. If not here, it belongs to the time of Sennacherib (705–681).

The death of Sargon in 705 and the accession of Sennacherib were naturally marked by new attempts to throw off the Assyrian overlordship. Merodach-baladan was ultimately defeated and expelled by Sennacherib, but the west gave much more trouble. Hezekiah came to the front by action against the Philistines, i.e., against a province of Assyria: 'He rebelled against the king of Assyria and served him not. He smote the Philistines unto Gaza and the borders thereof.' (2 Kings 18:7, 8.) He strengthened Jerusalem by a new underground water-supply (20:20, cf. 2 Chron. 32:30), probably that running through the tunnel of the famous Siloam inscription, and constituting a remarkable piece of engineering for those days. The miners worked from both ends, and the inscription signalizes the happy moment when the two tunnels met and became one:

'Whilst yet there were three cubits to be bored through, there was heard the voice of each calling to his fellow, for there was a split in the rock on the right hand . . . And on the day of the boring through the miners struck, each to meet his fellow, pick upon pick; and the waters flowed from the source to the pool for two hundred and a thousand cubits; and a hundred cubits was the height of the rock above the head of the miners.'[1]

The tunnel runs a circuitous course for 586 yards, with various corrections of direction, from the Virgin's Spring on

[1] Translation by G. A. Cooke, *North Semitic Inscriptions*, p. 15, cf. Pritchard, *A.N.E.T.* p. 321.

the east of the temple-hill to the Pool of Siloam within the walls of the old city, and the height increases from two and a half feet to sixteen feet at the lower and inner end.

In Ekron the rebellion broke out by a rising of the inhabitants against their governor Padi, who was handed over as a captive to Hezekiah. To meet this challenge, Sennacherib marched down the Phoenician and Philistine coasts, taking a number of towns, though not the impregnable Tyre. Finally he met and defeated an Egyptian and Ethiopian force at Eltekeh. As for Judah, he ravaged the Shephelah, capturing forty-six towns, and besieged Jerusalem, though he ultimately withdrew without capturing it. There is some difficulty in reconciling the Assyrian and Biblical sources, though both are agreed that Hezekiah submitted and paid a heavy tribute. There are two Biblical narratives of a 'prophetic' character, describing the Assyrian challenge to Jerusalem, which called for its surrender.[1] In both Isaiah declares that the city will not be taken, and that Sennacherib will withdraw; the more likely of the two narratives says because of the approach of the Ethiopians, the less likely because of a supernatural visitation of the Assyrian camp. It is disputed whether the challenge preceded or followed the payment of the tribute.

We are fortunate in having a number of contemporary prophecies by Isaiah, which take us inside Jerusalem during those exciting years that culminated in Sennacherib's siege of it. There is no hesitation in the prophet's condemnation of the social and religious conditions of his times; we may read it in what is now the opening chapter of his book. He is equally clear about the imminence and intensity of the danger from Assyria; he pictures the advance of the enemy on Jerusalem from the north, by describing the alarm of the villages and towns, one after another, as the news comes of the Assyrian approach, an approach almost as swift as the

[1] The Assyrian record will be found in Pritchard, *A.N.E.T.* pp. 287 f. With this, 2 Kings 18:13–16, is in fair agreement. The two 'prophetic' narratives are (i) 18:17–19:9a, 36b, 37, and (ii) 19:9b–36.

news itself.[1] The siege is pictured in 29; the city will be
brought to its lowest state. Then shall come the sudden
change to be wrought by the intervention of Yahweh: 'and
the multitude of all the nations that fight . . . against her
and her stronghold and distress her, shall be as a dream, a
vision of the night' (29:7). Elsewhere (17:13), he describes
them as chased away, 'as the chaff of the mountains before
the wind, and like the whirling dust before the storm'. This
faith rests essentially on the confidence that the maintenance
of Jerusalem is inseparable from the purpose of Yahweh:
'Behold I lay in Zion a stone for a foundation . . .; he that
hath faith shall not be put to shame' (cf. LXX of 28:16).
Judgment shall surely fall on the sinners of Jerusalem, and
only a sifted remnant of them will stand the test of that
judgment; but there is a definite limit to that which the
Assyrians shall be permitted to do, as the rod of God's anger,
the staff of his indignation (10:5). Just because Assyria has
exceeded that limit will he himself be brought to nought. It is
because of this supreme confidence in the purpose of Yahweh[2]
that Isaiah can dismiss with courteous detachment the envoys of the Ethiopians (18); what need of Egypt's help when
Yahweh is enthroned aloft in the heavens, hidden as in the
blaze of light of a summer noon, and waiting only for the
time of the harvest (vv. 4, 5)? To the people of Jerusalem he
pours forth his scorn on Egyptian aid, for the Egyptians are
but flesh, and Yahweh is spirit (31:3). Once more we hear the
primary insistence on faith as man's only wisdom in such
times: 'For thus said the Lord God, the Holy One of Israel,
In returning and rest shall ye be saved; in quietness and in
confidence shall be your strength: and ye would not' (30:15).

---

[1] 10:28-32; this is not a description of any actual advance; the
Assyrians actually advanced from Philistia.

[2] Isaiah's 'policy' is well described by Kittel (*Geschichte des Volkes
Israel*,[5] Vol. II, p. 489): 'Before his eyes there hovers the vision of
small and modest state under Assyrian supremacy, but as compensation
for the lost freedom he expects the much greater good of the gathering of
the pious and the building up of the kingdom of God in Jerusalem, until
the kingdom of the world falls of itself and the new kingdom (the Messia-
(nic will base itself on the corner-stone in Zion and on righteousness.'

The last glimpse of Jerusalem which we get from the prophet is the most striking of all (22). It describes the city as 'wholly gone up to the house-tops' to exult in the raising of the siege, 'full of shoutings, a tumultuous city, a joyous town', because of the reaction from the previous terror. 'In that day did the Lord, Yahweh of hosts, call to weeping and to mourning and to baldness and to girding with sackcloth: and behold, joy and gladness, slaying oxen and killing sheep, eating flesh and drinking wine.' Thus does the great prophetic interpreter of the history of his day utter his verdict on those who were blind to its meaning: 'ye looked not unto Him that had done this, neither had ye respect unto Him that fashioned it long ago.' With truth has it been said of Isaiah that his figure stands like a great statue, whilst the names of his contemporaries are but the inscription on its pedestal.

So far nothing has been said of the reformation of religion ascribed to Hezekiah (2 Kings 18:4). It is said that 'he removed the high places and brake up the *maṣṣeboth* and cut down the Asherah and crushed the bronze serpent which Moses made; for unto those days were the Israelites sacrificing to it, and it was called Nechushtan'. This anticipation of the reformation of Josiah seems to be confirmed by *v.* 22, where the Assyrian commander taunts Hezekiah with having dishonoured Yahweh by so doing: 'if ye say unto me, we trust in Yahweh our God: is not that he whose high places and whose altars Hezekiah hath taken away, and hath said to Judah and to Jerusalem, Ye shall worship before this altar in Jerusalem?' This verse would also imply that the reformation took place earlier in the reign of Hezekiah than the times of Sennacherib. But it is difficult to think that Hezekiah carried out such a centralization of religion in Jerusalem as did Josiah, for that would have gone far beyond anything contemplated by Isaiah, whose polemic was against idols, not the local sanctuaries.[1] On the other hand, it is quite

[1] Against the historicity of the statement, Stade, *Geschichte des Volkes Israel*, I, p. 607; for it, Kittel, *op. cit.*, p. 476, and Sellin, *Geschichte des israelitisch-jüdischen Volkes*, I, p. 270.

probable that Hezekiah did remove the Nechushtan, perhaps as a result of Isaiah's teaching. That might be the nucleus for a wider inference, and that inference may have been supported by the undoubted fact that Sennacherib's invasion must have destroyed many of the local sanctuaries, whilst the deliverance of Jerusalem gave it a new significance in the eyes of men.

4. Politics and Religion in the Seventh Century

The seventh century in the history of Judah begins with the withdrawal of Sennacherib from Jerusalem in 701 and ends (for the purposes of history) with the death of Josiah at Megiddo in 608. It is a century of strong religious contrasts, for it includes the heathen reaction under Manasseh and the reformation of religion under Josiah. It is also a century of great political events, which culminate in the fall of Nineveh in 612. The religion and the politics are, as usual, closely connected.

For the first decade of the century (to 687) Hezekiah remained king of Judah, though Judah had shrunk to little more than Jerusalem. Its condition at this time is pictured in part of the opening chapter of the prophecies of Isaiah (vv. 7, 8): 'Your country is desolate; your cities are burned with fire; your land, strangers devour it in your presence, and it is desolate, as the overthrow of strangers. And the daughter of Zion is left as a booth in a vineyard, as a lodge in a garden of cucumbers, as a besieged city.' We know hardly anything of this decade, and the religious reformation previously ascribed to Hezekiah may possibly have fallen within it, as a result of the actual destruction of the local sanctuaries by the Assyrians and the survival of Jerusalem, which vindicated Isaiah's faith. At any rate, Jerusalem was now necessarily unable to interfere in world politics, and free to pursue that purely religious mission which he had so earnestly advocated. This mission, cherished by a minority, was eventually to find expression in the Deuteronomic Reformation, towards which the reforms attributed to Hezekiah were an initial step.

With the accession of Manasseh in 687, however, there came a new development, in the revival of popular cults, and the official recognition of worship other than that of Yahweh. The causes for this reaction are obvious enough—on the one hand, the impossibility of keeping the common man on the high level of such a faith as Isaiah's, and on the other, the inevitable tendency of a state paying tribute to Assyria, and existing only on its sufferance, to recognize the worship practised by its sovereign. Through the first half of the century the power of Assyria was supreme. Sennacherib in 681 was succeeded by his son Esarhaddon (681–669), who re-asserted the Assyrian power over Babylon. In 677 he had to reduce a Syrian revolt which centred in Sidon, but he failed to take Tyre. Manasseh of Judah remained his vassal, with many other small kings of Syria. There is no Assyrian confirmation of the account of Manasseh's capture and imprisonment in Babylon given in 2 Chron. (33:10–13), though not in Kings. It is, of course, conceivable that Manasseh may have been engaged in some rebellion against Esarhaddon or his successor, Ashurbanipal (668–625), but it is more likely that the Chronicler inferred on religious grounds that some punishment must have befallen so wicked a king. Esarhaddon invaded Egypt in 009, and his son Ashurbanipal held Egypt for a short time; for the first half of the century Egypt was certainly not in a position to challenge the power of Assyria, and there can have been no pro-Egyptian party amongst the people of Jerusalem. Manasseh, indeed, with the other Syrian kings, had to contribute troops to the expedition of Ashurbanipal against Tirhakah. This may have led to the settlement of the Jewish military colony in Elephantine, and seems to explain the later words of Dt. 17:16, that Judah's king shall not cause the people to return to Egypt.

The features of the heathen reaction under Manasseh are described in 2 Kings 21:3–6. Here the reference to 'the host of heaven' is to the astral cult of Assyria and Babylonia; it implies the recognition of the religion of the suzerain. The

Baal and Asherah, here connected with Ahab's introduction
of Jezebel's religion from Phoenicia (1 Kings 16:32, 33),
probably cover the whole Canaanite cult of the fertility
goddess Ishtar, Astarte, and her male consort; the Phoenician
Baal was Melkart. The cult of the dead and magical usages
were a more or less permanent element in the popular
religion, reviving from time to time, much like modern
spiritualism. The sacrifice of children as a burnt-offering
may be compared with that made by Ahaz.[1] The high places
are the local sanctuaries throughout Judah, which were
probably destroyed in the time of Sennacherib's invasion. It
will be seen that all these features are no new inventions,
but the revival of practices already existent in other nations
or in the previous generations of Israel. They did not denote
in theory any abandonment of Yahweh as the God of Israel;
He simply became one member, though the most important,
of a pantheon. The 'innocent blood' which Manasseh is said
to have shed is doubtless that of the ardent Yahwists, the
disciples of the great prophets, who refused to countenance
this syncretistic system.

The prophet Zephaniah, who belongs to the period immediately after the long reign of Manasseh, gives us a cross-
section of the religious conditions in Judah at that time,
which the approaching 'Day of Yahweh' will judge and
remove; 'I will cut off the remnant of Baal from this place,
and the name of the Chemarim (idolatrous priests) with the
priests (of Yahweh who have been unfaithful to Him), and
them that worship the host of heaven upon the housetops,
and them that worship, which swear to Yahweh and swear
by Malcam (Milcom of the Ammonites or the Phoenician
Molech?), and them that are turned back from following
Yahweh (i.e., the syncretists and the indifferent)' (1:4–6).
He also indicates that these degenerate cults were recognized
and encouraged from above downwards; they were largely
due to the court and to political motives: 'in the day of
Yahweh's sacrifice, I will punish the princes and king's sons,

[1] 2 Kings 16:3. Cf. Micah, 6:6, 7.

and all such as are clothed with foreign apparel' (*v.* 8). Such
were the conditions in the days of Amon, the son of Manasseh,
who reigned for two years only (642–640) and was assassinated, possibly by members of a reforming party. That is
suggested by the fact that the assassins were themselves
killed by 'the people of the land' (2 Kings 21:23, 24), i.e., as it
would seem, by those satisfied with the existing conditions.

It is clear that reformation was due, if the genuine religion
of the prophets was to be continued at all. Political events
were occurring that made reformation possible. The great
Assyrian Empire had reached its highest development of
civilization under Ashurbanipal (668–625), but its military
power had become exhausted. The beginning of the end was
already to be discerned by such a prophet as Zephaniah,
who, like Jeremiah, seems to have been called into action by
the appearance of the Scythians (628–626). Herodotus
(1:105) tells us of an invasion of Assyrian territory, which
passed through Syria as far as Egypt, made by these hordes
of nomads from the north-east. Egypt had become independent again from 652. On the death of Ashurbanipal in
625, Nabopolassar made himself king of Babylon. Another
enemy of Assyria was Cyaxares of Media. Assyria, greatly
weakened by civil wars, was becoming quite unable to maintain its hold upon its outlying provinces, and this is what gave
Josiah his opportunity, not only to reform religion in Judah,
but to assert himself even in Samaria, and ultimately to make
an attempt, even against Egypt, to assert the independence of
his people. In this attempt, so far as the religious programme
was concerned, we may believe that an important part
belonged to the disciples of the eighth-century prophets and
the priests of Jerusalem who remained loyal to Yahweh-
worship.

The reformation began with the discovery of 'the book of
the law' in the temple, at a time when certain repairs were
being carried out. This book was handed by Hilkiah the
priest to Shaphan the king's 'Secretary of State', who in
turn delivered it to the king. It made a deep impression upon

him, and after consulting the prophetess Huldah, he read this 'book of the covenant' to the people, and entered into a covenant before Yahweh to obey its teaching.

The details of the reformation are given in 2 Kings 23:4–15. They follow fairly closely the items of Manasseh's syncretism already given. The cults of Baal and Astarte and the astral Babylonian cult were destroyed, their priests being suppressed, together with the immoral cults of the *qedeshim* and *qedeshoth*;[1] the place of burnt-offerings to Molech in the Ge-Hinnom was defiled (the valley gave its name to the later Gehenna); the roof-altars in connection with astral worship were removed, the high places to the gods of Sidon, Moab and Ammon, on the Mount of Olives, were also defiled. Two new features are mentioned, namely 'the horses and chariots of the sun', and the high places of the satyrs, or goat-demons.[2] Spiritualistic and magical practices were also put down (*v.* 24). But the reformation also extended beyond Jerusalem; all the high places of Judah were defiled (*v.* 8) and their priests brought up to Jerusalem, though they were not allowed to officiate there, as Deut. 18:6 had enacted. The fact that the reformation extended to Bethel, i.e., beyond Judah into the province of Samaria, was possible owing to the decline of the Assyrian control, and Josiah must have had the upper hand there, or he would not have ventured later on to meet Pharaoh Neco at Megiddo, with a hostile province behind him. These drastic acts were followed by a celebration of the Passover in Jerusalem, instead of at the local sanctuaries now destroyed. According to the general verdict of Old Testament scholarship the book of the law or of the covenant on which this reformation was based is included in our present Book of Deuteronomy, and this book, demanding the purification and centralization of worship at Jerusalem, was itself the product of the prophetic teaching of the eighth century, working on the basis of the

---

[1] The names denote 'holy' men and women, engaged in ritual prostitution at the sanctuaries.

[2] This depends on reading *hasse 'irim* for *hashshe 'arim* in *v.* 8.

book of the covenant which we have in Exodus. Josiah must
have felt that Yahweh would not abandon a king and people
who had so earnestly tried to obey His requirements; such
faith seems needed to explain his political and military
venture at Megiddo. To understand this venture it is necessary to review the circumstances which led to and followed
the fall of Nineveh in 612.

Until 1923 it was believed that Nineveh, the capital of the
Assyrian Empire, fell in 606, and older books, of course, give
this date. But in that year a tablet in the British Museum
was deciphered by C. J. Gadd which for the first time gave
details of events from 616 to 609, and showed that Nineveh
fell in 612. In 616, Nabopolassar of Babylon was attacking
the Assyrians, who had the Egyptians for allies, but in the
campaigns of both this and the following year he was unsuccessful. In 614 the Medes joined with the Babylonians.
In 612 after a two and a half months' siege chiefly by the
Medes, Nineveh fell. The Assyrians re-established themselves
in Harran, but were driven from it by the allies in 610.
The tablet ends with the year 609, when the Assyrians, with
their allies, the Egyptians, were vainly trying to recapture
Harran. Our Biblical book of Nahum describes very drama-
tically the capture of the hated city (2 and 3), and is regarded
by some as a liturgical celebration of the event. The importance of this new knowledge is not merely in regard to the
date of the fall of Nineveh, but also in regard to the significance of the expedition of Pharaoh Neco in 608, which led
to the death of Josiah. According to 2 Kings 23:29, 'In his
(Josiah's) days Pharaoh-neco king of Egypt (609–594) went
up against the king of Assyria to the river Euphrates; and
king Josiah went against him; and he slew him at Megiddo,
when he had seen him.' On the ground of this statement, it
was assumed that Egypt was seizing the moment of Assyria's
weakness to gain territory. But Josephus had already told
us that Neco was going to fight against the Medes and the
Babylonians who had overthrown the dominion of the
Assyrians. The Gadd tablet confirms Josephus as giving the

true explanation of the Biblical reference. It is clear that the Egyptians in 608 were coming to the help of the Assyrians as before, no doubt because Egypt knew that she would be herself exposed to the attack of the Medes and Babylonians, if they destroyed Assyria utterly.

What then of Josiah? Why was he fighting against Egypt? It could not be because of any alliance with the Medes and Babylonians. We must suppose that his faith in the presence of Yahweh led him to think that the hour was come for Judah to win again her lost independence, or rather to maintain it, since Josiah seems to have been free to work his will both in Judah and in the former Assyrian province of Samaria for more than a decade past. That the death of Josiah and the overthrow of national confidence made a deep impression on Jerusalem is seen by the words of Jeremiah, contrasting his fate with that of his son (Shallum-Jehoahaz) who was eventually taken captive to Egypt (22: 10): 'Weep ye not for the dead, neither bemoan him; but weep sore for him that goeth away, for he shall return no more nor see his native country.' We are told of Josiah that 'his servants carried him in a chariot dead from Megiddo, and brought him to Jerusalem and buried him in his own sepulchre'.

5. THE FALL OF JUDAH

There is an impressive parallel between the fall of Samaria and the fall of Jerusalem which reminds us that history, after all allowance for the freedom of individual personality, is still in some degree a science, according to which like causes will produce like events. We saw that the northern kingdom had six kings within a score of years, of whom only one, Menahem, died a natural death. Similarly, of the last six kings of Judah, one only, Jehoiakim, escaped captivity or a death by violence (though he least deserved such an escape). We may also note that to the two prophets Hosea and Isaiah who had watched the decline and fall of Israel, one from within and one from without, there correspond the two prophets

Jeremiah and Ezekiel, one within and one without, who were
contemporaries of the fall of Jerusalem. The external powers
concerned with the fall of Samaria were Assyria in the fore-
ground and Egypt in the background; in the fall of Jerusalem, Assyria was replaced by Babylon, and Egypt retained
her usual rôle of the tempting serpent in the Eden of
Yahweh's people.

On the death of Josiah at Megiddo, there was an attempt
to continue his struggle for independence—at least this is
the most likely interpretation of the election of his son
Jehoahaz as king by 'the people of the land' in place of his
elder brother, Eliakim, who was probably already disposed to
submit to Egypt. But the attempt was short-lived, for
Neco made Jehoahaz a prisoner, sending him to Egypt,
where he died. He was replaced by his brother Eliakim,
under the new name of Jehoiakim (2 Kings 23:31ff.). A
heavy indemnity was levied upon the people, which Jehoiakim had to collect. We have a vigorous judgment of Jehoiakim from the prophet Jeremiah (22:13–19), which accuses
him of exacting forced labour for the satisfaction of his
luxurious tastes—a large house, with roof-chambers, panelled
with cedar and painted with vermilion. The prophet, in the
spirit of Amos, contrasts the rapacity and injustice of
Jehoiakim with the moderate tastes of Jehoiakim's father,
Josiah, who 'judged the cause of the poor and needy'.

But Jeremiah had a larger and more serious indictment to
bring. The death of Josiah, and the subsequent loss of that
independence which the reformation seemed to have brought,
must have provoked a general religious reaction from the
stricter Yahwism. In an address that purports to have been
delivered in the first year of Jehoiakim's reign (26:1),
Jeremiah accuses Jerusalem of practising the cult of the
Babylonian Ishtar: 'The children gather wood, and the
fathers kindle the fire, and the women knead the dough,
to make cakes to the queen of heaven, and to pour out
drink-offerings unto other gods' (7:18). Worship on the
high places seems to have returned (13:27), and we know

from Ezekiel later on, how many pagan practices were included in the reaction from the Josianic Reformation, including the secret worship of animals, according to the Egyptian cult (Ezek. 8:10). It would seem that the two political parties, pro-Babylonian and pro-Egyptian, who make the warp and the woof of Judah's story in these generations, each pursued politics religiously in the sense of encouraging the cults of the countries towards which they looked. On the other hand, Jeremiah's 'temple sermon', as it is called (7 and 26), at the beginning of Jehoiakim's reign, attacks that blind reliance on the sure possession of Yahweh's sanctuary which was the illegitimate offspring of Isaiah's faith and Josiah's reformation.

As we have seen, Jehoiakim began to reign under the auspices of Egypt in 608, but this *regime* was short-lived, since Pharaoh Neco was disastrously defeated at Carchemish by Nebuchadrezzar, the son and soon the successor of Nabopolassar. This was in 605, but Nebuchadrezzar seems to have been too occupied with events further east, such as securing his succession to his father, to be able to deal with Syria. Jehoiakim may, therefore, have enjoyed some years of practical independence as a result of the battle of Carchemish (2 Kings 24:7).

It was not till about 601 that Nebuchadrezzar was free to turn his attention to Palestine; as a result of the appearance of the Babylonian armies, Jehoiakim became subject to him for three years (2 Kings 24:1), but then rebelled. Again Nebuchadrezzar was unable to deal directly with him, but employed guerilla bands from Edom,[1] Moab and Ammon, in conjunction with his own Syrian garrisons. Before Nebuchadrezzar himself arrived, Jehoiakim died a natural death, and his son, Jehoiachin, at the age of eighteen, succeeded to an inheritance of trouble. His reign lasted three months only; on the arrival of the Babylonian king to join his besieging army, Jehoiachin surrendered with his mother, his wives, his household, and his civil and military officers.

[1] So read with the Syriac, instead of 'Aram'.

He was taken as a prisoner to Babylon, and his imprisonment lasted for thirty-five years, until the death of Nebuchadrezzar, whose successor restored him to comparative liberty,
with recognition of his former status. In the long list of
deposed kings which history has provided, few can have been
more unfortunate; the restoration of outward respect to a
broken man in the fifties must have seemed a mocking
memorial of those far-off three months of harassed kingship
as a youth in a beleaguered city. Yet future generations did
not forget that his voluntary surrender saved the city from
destruction for another decade. Josephus (*Jewish War*, VI,
ii, 1) writes of him six centuries and a half afterwards in
enthusiastic strains. Nebuchadrezzar treated the city with
comparative leniency. There are inconsistent statements as
to the number deported (see p. 98), this being given as
10,000, 8,000 and 3,023 (2 Kings 24:14, 16, and Jer. 52:28),
but it is clear that Nebuchadrezzar removed the more sub-
stantial people, in the hope of making another revolt impossible, a hope that proved fallacious.

In place of Jehoiachin, as king of this enfeebled state,
Nebuchadrezzar set Jehoiachin's uncle, Mattaniah, with the
changed name of Zedekiah (the change of name denoting the
supremacy of him who changed it). The uncle was but three
years older than the nephew whom he displaced, and throughout his reign showed a weak character, which made him
yield to the influence of others. Apparently he was compelled
to swear an extraordinary oath of allegiance to Babylon,
since Ezekiel long afterwards blames him for his breach of it
(17:13 ff.).

The first movement of revolt occurred in the fourth year
of the reign of Zedekiah (594), and proved abortive. The
occasion seems to have been the coming of envoys to Zedekiah
from Edom, Moab, Ammon, Tyre and Sidon, to gain the
support of Judah in a common rebellion against Babylon.
Jeremiah was moved to declare, both by word of mouth, and
by the prophetic symbolism of a wooden yoke which he
bore, that the yoke of Babylon rested on the shoulders of all

the peoples by the will of Yahweh, and that it was useless to try to break it. A rival prophet, Hananiah, contradicted this, also in two-fold manner, for he broke the wooden yoke on Jeremiah's shoulders, and promised a return of the captives and of the captured vessels of the sanctuary within two years. For the moment the prophet Jeremiah was put to silence; but a subsequent oracle authorized him to make an iron yoke, and to denounce Hananiah as a false prophet (Jer. 27 and 28). In the same sense, Jeremiah wrote a letter to the exiles in Babylon, bidding them settle down for a couple of generations (29). The movement of revolt came to nothing, though it is possible that Zedekiah came under suspicion, and was summoned to Babylon to give an account of himself (Jer. 51:59).

The rebellion which issued in the second captivity and the fall of Jerusalem began in 588, when a new Pharaoh, Hophra (Apries), came to the throne and gave support. Ezekiel says that Zedekiah took the initiative in applying to him for horses and men (17:15). Ammon also was concerned, and Ezekiel gives a dramatic picture of Nebuchadrezzar taking the omens at the parting of the ways which led to Ammon and Judah respectively, as to which he should reduce first (21:18ff.). The lot fell for Judah and Jerusalem. The siege of Jerusalem lasted eighteen months,[1] and there was a revival of hope when the approach of an Egyptian army compelled the temporary raising of the siege (Jer. 37:5). But the respite was brief; Hophra was defeated, and the siege resumed. There were bitter sufferings within, through famine and its accompanying horrors, which are described in the first chapter of the 'Lamentations'. Finally a breach was made in the walls and the position became hopeless. Zedekiah attempted flight, but was captured at Jericho, taken to Riblah, and blinded after seeing his sons killed. Jeremiah for his part had narrowly escaped with his life during the

---

[1] 'The Lachish Letters' (ed. by H. Torczyner, 1938) belong to this period, and illustrate military conditions at Lachish and Azekah (cf. Jer. 34:6, 7).

siege, being hated because of his consistent policy of surrender.

After a month the Babylonian general in command received orders to destroy all that could be destroyed, and to deport the inhabitants, except that the lowest classes were left to carry on agriculture. A number of the leading men were executed at Riblah. All metal objects of value were taken. Gedaliah, a Judaean, was left as governor over those who remained. But he was treacherously assassinated by Ishmael, a prince of Davidic blood, with the support of Ammon, and those who had supported Gedaliah thought it safest to take refuge in Egypt, whither they carried Jeremiah, notwithstanding his protests.

Thus ended the history of Judah as a political state, never to be resumed as such, except for the Hasmonaean kingship in the century prior to the Roman domination. But Jeremiah had rightly discerned that the hope of the future lay with the exiles in Babylon, and for him it was a real hope. The political life of Judah was no such loss as it seemed, since it had already served its purpose—that of nurturing and developing a religious faith, destined to grow into a world religion.

VI.—THE EXILIC PERIOD

1. The Political Background

THE period known as the Exile extends for about half a century, from the destruction of Jerusalem in 586 to the Edict of Cyrus permitting Jews to return to their native land. The political background is clear and simple in its main features. Egypt does not seem to have interfered in the affairs of Syria, though Tyre held out against the Babylonians for thirteen years till 573. Nebuchadrezzar was able to devote much of his energy to temple-building, of which remarkable evidences remain. He reigned till 562, when he was succeeded by three rulers of very short reigns. The first of these alone concerns us; it was the Amel-Marduk (Biblical Evil-merodach) who set Jehoiachin free in 561 (2 Kings 25: 27–30). In 556 the last ruler of the Neo-Babylonian Empire, Nabonidus, began to reign. He was a scholar and an archaeologist elected by the influential priesthood,[1] but later on he wholly alienated the priests on religious grounds, and this greatly contributed to his overthrow and with it that of the empire. The aged king spent much of his time at Teima in Arabia, and his son Belshazzar was in charge of affairs. The overthrow of the Empire came through Cyrus, who in 553 revolted against Astyages and became king of the united Medes and Persians (closely related peoples of Aryan stock). Cyrus then proceeded to conquer Croesus, the dominant power in Asia Minor, whom he overthrew at Sardes in 546.

[1] There is evidence to suggest that Nabonidus was not at Teima primarily for archaeological research, but as a political measure to keep open one of the trade routes to the south (the other being controlled by Egypt). See S. Smith, *Isaiah, Chapters XL-LV*, 1944, pp. 36 ff.

In that year he began operations against Babylon, but these were not carried through before 539, in which year he conquered Belshazzar, whilst his general Gobryas received the surrender of Babylon without any fighting there. Gobryas was made governor, and Cyrus reconciled his new subjects to the change by wise toleration.

2. THE SOCIAL AND RELIGIOUS CONDITIONS IN JUDAEA

As to the number of Jews exiled in 597 and 586, inconsistent figures are given. In the earlier deportation, it would seem that from eight to ten thousand *men* of the better classes were taken (2 Kings 24:14–16), so as to hinder any further revolt. Jer. 52:28 ff. gives 3,023 as the number, and adds figures for 586 (and for another deportation in 582), which seem much too small. In Sennacherib's days, the whole population of Judaea may have been a quarter of a million, since he claims to have taken captive 200,150 in all (a figure which excludes Jerusalem). In 586, the population was probably less. The total number of exiles is likely to have been much smaller than those who were left in Judaea (cf. Ezek. 33:24); Guthe estimates the exiles at about 12,000 men,[1] together with women and children—say 36,000–48,000 in all. At any rate, the whole subsequent history seems to show that Judaea was very far from being depopulated or from lying waste and uncultivated, and there is ample evidence that it was soon recruited by the inflow of surrounding peoples.

As to the social conditions in Judaea, the evidence of the genealogies in Chronicles, combined with an examination of the geography of places named in the later history, suggests that a number of clans from the Negeb, the 'Southland', moved northwards, and were now or later incorporated with the Jews, viz., the Kenites, Kenizzites, Calebites and Jerachmeelites. These may have been under pressure from the Edomites, and the Edomites themselves under pressure from the nomads, as they certainly were at a later time from

[1] *Geschichte des Volkes Israel,*[3] p. 267.

the Nabataean Arabs. Further, we have evidence that
Ammonites were concerned in the new conditions in Judaea,
for the assassination of Gedaliah through Ishmael was
prompted and supported by the Ammonite king, whilst in
the time of Nehemiah we find Tobiah the Ammonite in
marriage-alliance with the chief priest and actually having
quarters in the temple precincts (Neh. 13:4, 5); there had
been extensive marriage of Jews with Philistines, Ammonites
and Moabites (13:23). All this points to a very mixed
population in Judaea, and explains the low religious conditions of this period and later. Politically, there must have
been a Babylonian governor to replace Gedaliah, and a
suitable organization of officers under him, unless the territory was administered from the province of Samaria, as is
possible. Socially, there must have been at first great
poverty, but a class of the 'new rich' soon began to come
into being, by the occupation and cultivation of lands of
which previous owners had been dispossessed. By the end of
the exile there must have been a very considerable population, different in outlook from the exiles. The exiles belonged
on the whole to the better classes, socially and religiously,
and this helps to explain subsequent developments.

The religious conditions in Judaea can be illustrated in
several ways. In a country under Babylonian rule, with
foreign officers, there must have been every encouragement
for the official Babylonian cults. Already in the narrative
of events in connection with Gedaliah and the flight to
Egypt of a considerable number of Jews, we find Jeremiah
protesting in Egypt against the cult of the 'Queen of Heaven',
i.e., Ishtar (Jer. 44:18, 19). Ezekiel, who was one of those
deported in 597,[1] testified as to the condition of things in the
temple before 586; the 'image of jealousy' (8:3) was probably
that of Ishtar, whilst Tammuz, for whom he saw women
weeping, is the Babylonian equivalent of the Phoenician
Adonis (v. 14). He also saw the Egyptian animal-worship

[1] Or possibly not until 586, a view to which Robinson himself adhered
at a later date, see his book, *Two Hebrew Prophets*, 1948, p. 76. L.H.B.

being carried on in a secret chamber. At the same time, the worship of the old Canaanite Baalim was reinforced from Samaria, as we may see from certain chapters towards the end of our Book of Isaiah, which probably belong to this period, and refer to Judaea (57:3–8; 65:3–5; 66:3, 17). The references in these passages are doubtless to that syncretism to which there was so steady a drift in Palestine; in the case of Jews it would not mean the entire abandonment of the worship of Yahweh, but the combination of that worship with other cults and practices drawn from alien religions. Certainly these protests against such syncretism suggest that genuine Yahweh-worshippers remained in Judaea, as is also shown by the account of the eighty pilgrims coming from Shechem, Shiloh and Samaria to bring offerings to the now ruined house of Yahweh (Jer. 41:4f.). This proves that worship continued after 586 on the site of the temple, whose visible desolation, together with the inner desolation of the devout, is so movingly described in certain of the Lamentations (esp. chapters 1 and 5). That these Yahweh-worshippers in Judaea shared in the thoughts and hopes of those in Babylon may be seen from the prophecies of Isaiah 21, which anticipate the fall of Babylon, and emanate in all probability from Judaea.

3. THE EXILES IN BABYLON

It is misleading to think of the Jewish exiles in Babylon as being in 'captivity'. Their position seems to have been that of recognized foreigners, affiliated to the plebeian class of citizens and naturally without the privileges of the Babylonian aristocracy, but distinctly higher in status than the slave-class. This position of comparative freedom seems to be presupposed by the letter which Jeremiah sent to them, urging them to settle down peacefully, and live the ordinary life of citizens (29:5–7):

'Build ye houses and dwell in them; and plant gardens and eat the fruit of them; take ye wives and beget sons and

daughters; and take wives for your sons, and give your
daughters to husbands, that they may bear sons and
daughters; and multiply ye there, and be not diminished.
And seek the peace of the city whither I have caused you
to be carried away as exiles, and pray unto Yahweh for it;
for in the peace thereof shall ye have peace.'

Instead of 'the city' we should probably read with the
Septuagint 'the land', since the Jews were for the most part
agriculturalists, and would find their living in work in the
fields, especially at first. Later on, the more able amongst
them no doubt penetrated into the towns, and engaged in
commerce. It is noteworthy that Ezekiel describes Babylon
as 'a land of traffic . . . a city of merchants', and this is
perhaps the point at which the national genius for business
first began to show itself. In the next century we have
evidence of Jewish traders in Babylon, and the fact that
Nehemiah, a Jew, could attain a position of high confidence
with the king is itself significant. That the Jews were able to
acquire wealth in Babylon in the course of half a century,
though they must have started without any resources, shows
again their relative independence. When the time for return
came, the patriotic Jews were able to contribute very liberally
to the projected restoration of the temple (Ezra 2:69). We
further hear, about twenty years later, of contributions sent
from Babylon to Jerusalem (Zech. 6:9ff.). All this pre-
supposes tolerant treatment on the part of the Babylonian
rulers, always excepting the attitude to political agitators,
such as the two prophets mentioned by Jeremiah (29:21ff.)
who were burnt to death, presumably for treasonable utter-
ances, e.g., proclamation of the speedy downfall of Babylon.

The relative freedom enjoyed by the Jews in Babylon is
also seen in the fact that they were allowed to retain their
own organization, and that their groups were not broken up.
The Jewish elders visited and consulted Ezekiel (8:1; 14:1;
20:1), who was living as a married man (24:18) in his own
house (3:24; 12:3; cf. 33:30), at a place called Tel-abib

(3:15). There were other settlements of Jews in the neighbourhood (Ezra 8:15, 17), and there was evidently considerable freedom of intercourse amongst them. Registers
of the families were kept, which pre-supposes considerable
stability of social life (Ezek. 13:9; cf. Ezra 2:59-62; 8:1).
All this was destined to be of the greatest importance for the
future. When Sargon deported 27,290 inhabitants of Samaria
in 722, he seems to have scattered them in Northern Mesopotamia and Media (2 Kings 17:6), doubtless in order to
remove the possibility of any successful rebellion. The result
of this Assyrian policy was the merging of these northern
exiles into the life of their environment, without any trace of
them being left, whilst the importation of foreign colonists
into the northern kingdom not less successfully prevented
any common national basis, and helped to corrupt its religion.
But the exiles from Judaea, partly through the more tolerant
policy of Nebuchadrezzar, were able to retain their national
unity, and in fact to gain by their transplantation both
economically and religiously. They were now living in a
wealthy and prosperous land, and they were removed from
the Baalism of pre-exilic days in Canaan, and left free to
develop the moral and spiritual worship of Yahweh.

4. THE RELIGIOUS LIFE OF THE EXILES

What sort of religious life was there amongst these people?
Something of their attitude may be gathered from sayings of
theirs which Ezekiel quotes—and he knew them intimately
and critically. At first, there must have been the expectation
of a speedy deliverance by the hand of Yahweh, but as the
years passed and the sky did not lighten, they said 'The days
are prolonged and every vision faileth'; 'our bones are dried
up and our hope is lost' (12:22; 37:11). Those who found
moral and religious teaching in the course of events could
say, 'Our transgressions and our sins are upon us, and we
pine away in them' (33:10); but others were readier to say,
'The fathers have eaten sour grapes and the children's teeth
are set on edge' (18:2). There was readiness to hear what a

prophet had to say: 'Come, I pray you, and hear what is the word that cometh forth from Yahweh' (33:30); yet others bitterly said, 'The way of Yahweh is not equal' (18:25). We can see from such sayings just what we should expect—that there were many varieties of reaction to their misfortunes, and that our generalizations are hazardous. We can learn from both Jeremiah and Ezekiel that there were 'false prophets' amongst them (Jer. 29:21–3; Ezek 13:1–9; 14:5–10), and that idolatry continued (Ezek. 20:30–42; 14:3–9). The foreign land was religiously unclean (cf. Hos. 9:3–5; Amos 7:17; 2 Kings 5:17; Ezek. 4:13). They could not, therefore, practise the established ordinances of religion, which required the ordained place of sacrifice. But this very divorce from the common acts of worship already familiar led to the development of a religious individualism, which had already been inaugurated so nobly by Jeremiah's personal communion with God. It was still possible for the devout to pray—with the face turned towards Jerusalem (1 Kings 8:48). Fasting could in some degree replace sacrifice (Ezra 8:21; cf. Neh. 1:4). The spiritual offerings of a new heart and a new spirit, of which Ezekiel speaks (11:19; 36:26), could still be made, and these required no visible altar (cf. Ezek. 18:5–9 for the prophet's programme of a just man). The food-laws could be largely observed, as we see from Ezekiel's own example: 'from my youth up even till now have I not eaten of that which dieth of itself, or is torn of beasts; neither came there abominable flesh into my mouth' (4:14). The ancient practice of Sabbath observance now assumed a new importance (Ezek. 20:12–21; 22:8, 26; 23:38), and also a new character, as an act of self-denial, and a distinctive and characteristic mark of Judaism; so also was circumcision, amongst an uncircumcised people like the Babylonians. We cannot say exactly when and where the synagogue began, for the only possible reference to it in the Old Testament comes from a Maccabean psalm (74:8: 'they have burned up all the synagogues of God in the land'). But we can safely say that its foundations were laid in the

H

needs of exile, and that the study of the Scriptures, which was to become the distinctive feature of the synagogue, undoubtedly contributed at this time to maintain the religious spirit. It was indeed in this period that much of the Bible must have taken its present form. The new consciousness of sin, and the new need of atonement,[1] seen in the Book of Ezekiel were surely not confined to him; they are reflected in that subsequent development of ritual (in which Ezekiel himself was a pioneer) which warrants his title, 'the father of Judaism'. The two prophets of the Babylonian exile, Ezekiel and Deutero-Isaiah, can here receive no more than the barest notice. Ezekiel proclaims the self-revelation of the holy and glorious God in history, whether in wrath before 586, or subsequently in the restoration of the city and temple, and in the divine judgment on the nations. Men are individually responsible before God, and the power of His Spirit can alone change the evil hearts of men and restore the nation. The dominating thought of Ezekiel's vision of the future is seen in his closing word about the new Jerusalem: 'Yahweh is there.'

Another and quite different outlook on the future is seen in Deutero-Isaiah, whose prophecies accompany and interpret the striking career of Cyrus. This prophet also looks for divine and supernatural intervention, though mediated by human agency. He comforts the exiles with the promise of speedy deliverance, his hope being explicitly built on the power of Yahweh over nature, history and the unknown future. The sorrows of Israel will find a divine justification, not only by restoration to the homeland, but by a sacrificial significance which will convert the nations to the worship of Yahweh. He had far less influence on the immediate future than his fellow-prophet, but a far greater one on the ultimate development of religion, especially in the New Testament.

[1] Ezekiel orders two days of atonement, viz., on the first day of the first month and on the first day of the seventh month (LXX), see 45:18-20. The great Day of Atonement of Lev. 16 was on the tenth day of the seventh month, and was of post-exilic development.

5. CYRUS

A generation after the destruction of Jerusalem, i.e., about
the middle of the sixth century, there emerged the remarkable figure of Cyrus, who was to be so important a factor in
Israel's literature and history. Cyrus was the king of districts
east and north-east of the Persian Gulf, which were tributary
to the Medes, and were known as Anshan and Persia. The
Medes ruled the territory south of the Caspian Sea and right
across the north-west to the River Halys in Asia Minor
(flowing to the middle of the southern coast of the Black Sea).
They were now pressing into the northern part of Mesopotamia, where they captured Harran on a tributary of the
upper Euphrates. But a new movement on the flank of the
Medes checked their advance. In 553 their Persian vassal
Cyrus opened war upon them, and by 550 had conquered
them. His realm now extended from the country between
the Persian Gulf and the Caspian, right across the former
realm of Assyria, into Asia Minor. Here Croesus ruled over
Lydia. Against the Persian Cyrus Croesus allied himself with
Nabonidus of Babylon and Amasis of Egypt. But in 547 the
Persians defeated him at Pteria (near the Halys), and pressed
on to Sardes, his capital, which surrendered to Cyrus in 540
(cf. Herodotus i, 73 f.).

Cyrus had thus overthrown one of the three neighbouring
kingdoms, and Babylon lay next in his path. It was natural,
therefore, that Hebrew prophecy, alert to discern the signs
of the times, should begin to interpret the victories of Cyrus
in terms of its own religious faith. One of these interpreta-
tions, probably from Palestine, is to be found in Is. 21:1–10,
in which a series of four visions show Elam and Media about
to attack (2), the interrupted banquet of the Babylonians (5),
the advancing troops (7), the fall of Babylon (9). But the
noblest interpretation of the advance of Cyrus was given
about this time (41:2–4) by the prophet whom we call
Deutero-Isaiah, who seems to be writing in the period when
Cyrus was winning such impressive successes in Asia Minor.

The fulfilment of these great hopes did not come for some time, though Cyrus advanced as far as Erech on the lower Euphrates by 546; he was kept occupied with the neighbours on his eastern borders. Meanwhile the Babylonian king, Nabonidus, weakened his own position by incurring the hatred of his religious officials, through the displacement of Marduk in favour of other gods. In 539 the long threatened attack on Babylon was made. Cyrus came through Assyria, and defeated Nabonidus and his son, Belshazzar, at Opis on the Tigris. Nabonidus fled to Borsippa, and Babylon was captured without any serious resistance. Gobryas, who had gone over to the side of Cyrus, took possession of the city, and Cyrus followed him in. Gobryas seems to have followed 'Bel-sharusur' and killed him. The remarkable fact that so strong a city as Babylon should have surrendered so easily evidently impressed men, as we may see from the story of Daniel 5, and Herodotus i, 190f. Babylon was not however plundered or destroyed; Cyrus seems to have been welcomed as a deliverer, and made Babylon a place of residence. It is probable that Cyrus professed the Mazdean religion; we do not know how this affected his tolerant religious outlook.[1] According to the Cylinder of Cyrus,[2] he restored the place of the outraged Marduk, and gave back the Sumerian and Accadian gods, with their worshippers. Thus the edict (Ezra 6:1-5) affecting the return of the Jews, however re-

---

[1] 'The religion as it came from the prophet Zarathustra himself was *in*tolerant—perhaps the most intolerant of all ancient faiths, and when revived as state-religion by the Sassanids, it was again intolerant. Under Darius and onwards it had certainly re-admitted old popular gods, and some of foreign origin. But before that (e.g., under Cyrus) we really know nothing about it.' (A. J. D. Farrer, in a written communication.)

[2] For the Cylinder, see Pritchard, *A.N.E.T.* p. 316, esp. 'I returned . . . the images which used to live therein (i.e. territories near Babylon) and established for them permanent sanctuaries. I also gathered all their former inhabitants and returned to them their habitations. Furthermore I resettled upon the command of Marduk, the great lord, all the gods of Sumer and Akkad whom Nabonidus has brought into Babylon to the anger of the lord of the gods, unharmed in their former chapels, the places which make them happy.'

worded in its Jewish statement,[1] is quite in the line of his policy as known from other sources. The Aryan treatment of Israel was to contrast very favourably with that of its earlier Semitic rulers.

[1] Though probably nearer the original than that of Ezra 1.

VII.—THE JEWS UNDER THE PERSIANS
(539–333)

By the close of the exile, the monotheistic faith of Israel had been irrevocably established. It was that faith which raised a sufficient number of Jews from the grave of the exile to create the post-exilic community in Judaea. But the new *forms* of that faith—its stricter nationalism, the developed ritual of the second Temple, including the rich expression of praise and prayer in the Psalms, the application of prophetic principle to everyday morality in the Wisdom literature, the elaboration of apocalyptic eschatology, and of the definite doctrine of life beyond death—all these were to be wrought out largely through contact with the world-empires and their civilizations. This is what chiefly gives both unity and interest to the six centuries of history that remain, until the chosen people were to revert to the ancestral rôle of the wandering Aramaean, Jacob.

The important results for religion do not belong to the scope of this book; we are concerned with the external factors of the process of reaching them. The Persian, the Greek and the Roman each took his turn in unconscious ministry to the purpose of God. Those of them who tried to shatter the faith proved powerless to do this; but each left his mark on the forms of the faith or helped to shape the history which was its cradle. 'Essential Judaism possessed within itself a vitality and vigour which enabled it to maintain its central core unimpaired. The mere fact that it could assimilate so much without sacrificing its identity is a mark of power, and in this respect Judaism has more than vindicated itself.'[1] The great creative moments were past, but there was much chisel-work to be done on Judaism before another creation came into being alongside of it, not less the issue of the same history. Judaism and Christianity are the work of a single Sculptor, just as much as the twin statues of them in the porch of Strasbourg Cathedral.

1. THE 'RETURN' AND THE SECOND TEMPLE

The traditional account of the 'Return' is derived from the narrative of Ezra 1–6, compiled by the author of 'Chronicles', two or three centuries later. According to this account, some 50,000 Jews returned in one body from Babylon, after formal permission from Cyrus, and under Sheshbazzar, in 538. In the seventh month after their return they erected the altar at Jerusalem; in the second year, they laid the foundation of the Temple. But further work upon it was checked by the jealousy and accusations of 'the people of the land', and work was not resumed until the time of Darius (520). There are serious difficulties, however, in the way of accepting this account as historical, apart from the lack of any contemporary evidence. That Cyrus gave permission for such a return need not be doubted, as it agreed with his general policy in dealing with the subject nationalities (see p. 106), nor that some Jews may have availed themselves of it. On the other hand, when the actual rebuilding of the Temple began (520), the contemporary sources, viz., Haggai and Zechariah, show no knowledge of any previous attempt, or of any previous 'Return' on the scale depicted by the Chronicler. There are also numerous inconsistencies in the Chronicler's own account of the alleged 'Return' in 538, e.g., the confusion between Sheshbazzar[2] and Zerubbabel as the leader of the expedition, and the use of the Aramaic document contained in Ezra 4:8–24, which relates to the times of Artaxerxes (464–424), but is adduced to explain events

---

[1] G. H. Box, *Judaism in the Greek Period*, p. 68 (*Clarendon Bible*).
[2] He seems to be the Shenazzar of 1 Chron. 3:18, son of Jehoiachin and uncle of Zerubbabel.

alleged to have happened under Cyrus (538–529). The list of names in Ezra 2 (reproduced in Neh. 7) as those of returned exiles, more probably belongs to a census of much later date, e.g., of Nehemiah's time.[1] When we add the independent evidence of the Chronicler's free handling of early sources, it seems highly probable that he has been influenced by his belief that there must have been some spectacular fulfilment of the hopes of Deutero-Isaiah, and that he has ante-dated the events, gathering up a whole series of smaller 'returns' into one great caravan.

We are on solid ground when we use the contemporary evidence of Haggai and Zechariah. From Haggai it is clear that in the second year of Darius, i.e., 520, the Temple had not been re-built, and that there was no immediate intention to build it. There had been a considerable shortage of crops, owing to drought, and people said that the time was not fitting for such an undertaking. The prophet, on the contrary, assures them that the adversity shows the anger of Yahweh, directed against their unwillingness to build the Temple, whilst they can find resources to build their own houses. 'Build the Temple,' he says in effect, 'and Yahweh will give prosperity,' anticipating the words, 'Seek first the kingdom of God and His righteousness, and all these things shall be added unto you.' As a result of the prophet's words, Zerubbabel and Joshua, the secular and religious leaders, turned the people to the task, which was begun about three weeks afterwards. Apparently, it required three months of preparatory work before the foundation of the Temple could be laid (2:18), so that if anything had really been done in 537, it counted for little or nothing. Meanwhile Haggai combated the spirit of depression which came on those old men who remembered the Temple which had been destroyed sixty-seven years before. He did this by interpreting the political disturbances of Darius' first years as signs of the coming 'Messianic' upheaval, with its ultimate establishment

[1] So Guthe, *op. cit.*, pp. 295–6; cf. Lods, *The Prophets and the Rise of Judaism*, pp. 190–2.

of Yahweh's kingdom, and the flowing of the wealth of
the nations to the Temple (2:7, 21f.). Doubtless it was the
condition of the Persian empire that moved both him and
Zechariah to speak in the name of Yahweh. Cambyses had
committed suicide in 522, after confessing that he had
murdered his brother Smerdis. A large number of claimants
of the throne at once emerged, and Darius Hystaspis had to
overthrow no less than nine in different parts of the empire.
He overcame Babylon in 520, though its second revolt was
not subdued until 519. We can well understand, therefore,
that in 520 the prophets might expect the speedy downfall
of the Persian empire, and the coming of the Messianic age.
It was, in fact, the Messianic hope that built the second
Temple.

In accordance with this, Haggai declares that Zerubbabel
is to become God's 'signet' (2:23), i.e., to be given the royal
place from which his grandfather, Jehoiachin (Coniah in
Jer. 22:24, from which the metaphor is derived), had been
deposed. Zerubbabel is to be the Messiah, the anointed
Davidic prince. This is confirmed by Zechariah, who calls
him the 'Shoot' of David (6:12; cf. 4:7–9).[1] Perhaps the
hopes thus centred in the last of the Davidic line were the
cause of the sudden disappearance of Zerubbabel from
history, as sudden as that of his forerunner Sheshbazzar.
The authorities might permit the building of a temple, but
they were not likely to allow the governor of a petty district
to claim royal honours.

The account of the re-building of the Temple thus re-
constructed from the prophecies of Haggai and Zechariah
may be supplemented by what the Chronicler tells us, and in
particular by the episode of Tattenai, the Persian governor
of Syria. At some early stage in the proceedings he and his
officials visited Jerusalem to inquire into the authority for
the erection of this new building. They were referred to the

---

[1] Zech. 6:9 ff. has been obscured by an attempt to make the priesthood
the subject of the prophecy. The night-'visions' of Zechariah (1:7–6:8)
further develop the Messianic hope.

permission originally given by Cyrus, and they reported accordingly to the Persian court, with the result that the permission was confirmed by Darius, who, according to the Chronicler, made state-contributions to the cost of both the building and the sacrifices. The Chronicler also speaks of the completion and dedication of the Temple in 516, and of a subsequent celebration of the Passover.

On the contemporary evidence of Haggai and Zechariah, the building of the Temple was due to the initiative of returned exiles ('the remnant') assisted by 'the people of the land', from whom there was as yet no cleavage.[1] Later on, in the times of Nehemiah and Ezra, that cleavage came, and it is reflected in the still later account by the Chronicler of the hostility of 'the people of the land' as having operated from the beginning (Ezra 4:1-4).

2. NEHEMIAH AND EZRA

After the completion of the Temple in 516, there was a period of nearly three-quarters of a century about which we have no direct information at all, except for the Aramaic document in Ezra 4:8-24. Even the Chronicler is altogether silent about it. But light is thrown upon it indirectly by some of the prophecies known as Isaiah 56-66, Obadiah, *vv.* 1-14 and Malachi. The last, in particular, gives a valuable cross-section of the life of the Jewish community in the fifth century, shortly before the reforming work of Nehemiah and Ezra, which it abundantly justifies.

We must picture a small and decidedly impoverished group of people, living in an area not much more than twenty miles each way and poor in soil, though its inhabitants depended chiefly on agriculture. They enjoyed religious freedom under their Persian governor, but had lost their political

---

[1] The natural meaning of 'the remnant' is given by Is. 46:3; Zech. 8:6 shows that it could be used inclusively of all who shared in the work, and Haggai 2:2 suggests that it could be used to include 'the people of the land' (*v.* 4) who co-operated. In Ezra 6:21, 'all such as had separated themselves from the filthiness of the heathen of the land', we see how the transition from one group to the other could be made.

independence, and had to pay tribute. They complain of their religious and civil leaders; the prophets are called blind watchmen, dumb dogs who cannot bark, though they are greedy enough, and the rulers are shepherds without understanding, except for their own gain (Is. 56:9–12). These rulers figure as 'those that oppress the hireling in his wages, the widow and the fatherless, and that turn aside the resident alien from his right, and fear not Yahweh' (Mal. 3:5). It is evident that the disillusionment which followed the rebuilding of the Temple played havoc with religion and morality. The Temple was indeed there, however impoverished, but the walls of the city had not been built up, and no 'Messianic' age had dawned.

Scepticism was rife (Mal. 1:2; 2:17; 3:14, 15) and 'Malachi' protests against the indifference to organized religion, shown in the withholding of the tithes, and the offering of imperfect animals for the sacrifices, and also against the disloyalty with which Jews divorced their Jewish wives to contract more advantageous marriages with foreign women. The motives for this practice spring from the fact that the community was now closely surrounded by 'foreigners', with whom it was useful to have these marriage connections. Apart from the 'Samaritans', of whom particular mention will be made later on, there were Edomites, Ammonites, Philistines, etc. The Edomites, driven into Canaan by the pressure of the Nabataean Arabs, had occupied Jewish territory to the south, including Hebron. The bitterness felt against them is reflected in each of the documents named—Obadiah, Malachi (1:2–5) and Is. 63:1–6. Tobiah the Ammonite appears in the time of Nehemiah as a leader against the Jews. The Philistine opposition is represented by that of Sanballat's Ashdolite supporters (Neh. 4:7). In view of all these unfavourable conditions both within and without the Jewish community, we see more clearly the importance of the fact that a minority remained faithful to the old ideals, and waited for the judgment of Yahweh on a faithless and perverse generation: 'they that feared Yahweh spake one with another: and Yahweh hearkened and heard, and a book of remembrance was written before Him' (Mal. 3:16). With this minority, when once more reinforced from Babylon, the future lay.

It was probably towards the end of this period that the Jews undertook that building of the walls which is mentioned in Ezra 4:12. But this attempt served only to arouse official suspicions, and Artaxerxes (464–425) ordered it to cease. It may have been this particular setback which stirred the patriotic Nehemiah to action. He occupied a post which brought him into personal contact with the king, of whom he seems to have been a favourite. He employed his influence to secure his own appointment as governor of Judaea, with authority to deal with the situation. This change of policy on the part of Artaxerxes agrees with what is known of his character from other sources, as being easily influenced by those in personal contact with him. According to the narrative of the Chronicler, Nehemiah had been preceded in 458 by Ezra (Ezra 7:7). But there are good reasons for placing Ezra *after* Nehemiah. (*a*) None of those named as returning with Ezra (Ezra 8:1–14) are mentioned as helping Nehemiah to build the walls of Jerusalem (Neh. 3). (*b*) The original 'memoirs' of both Nehemiah and Ezra represent each as working independently, with no mention of the work of the other.[1] (*c*) Ezra 9:9, however, pre-supposes the work of Nehemiah, for it mentions not only the building of the ruined Temple but also that of the wall.[2] (*d*) Nehemiah forbids the marriage of Jews with foreign women in future but does not require existent marriages of the kind to be cancelled (Neh. 13:23 ff.). Ezra requires Jews to divorce

[1] The name of Nehemiah occurs in Neh. 8:9, but is absent from the Greek Ezra (9:49); there is a difference also in Neh. 10:1, whilst 12:26, 36, belong to the Chronicler. It is probable that Neh. 8–10 belongs to the 'memoirs' of Ezra, at least in part.

[2] It is not certain whether the word is to be taken literally or figuratively: it is not the normal word for a city wall. For a full discussion of the Ezra–Nehemiah problem see H. H. Rowley's essay, 'The Chronological Order of Ezra and Nehemiah' in *The Servant of the Lord*, 1952.

their foreign wives (Ezra 10:3ff.), a much more drastic action, explicable after the failure of the first, but less easily before it. (e) The Elephantine papyri (see p. 122) show that Jochanan was high priest in 408[1]; now Jochanan (or Jehochanan) was a contemporary of Ezra (Ezra 10:6) and the *grandson* (Neh. 12:11, where called 'Jonathan') of Eliashib,[2] the contemporary of Nehemiah (Neh. 13:4, 7, 28). In view of all this, and of other evidence, we should certainly place the work of Ezra after that of Nehemiah. The simplest assumption is that 'in the seventh year of Artaxerxes' (Ezra 7:7) referred originally to the *second* king of that name (404–358), so that Ezra came to Jerusalem in 397.[3] The Chronicler may have placed him before Nehemiah under the influence of a natural inclination to give priority to the work of the priest over that of the secular governor.

Nehemiah was governor of Jerusalem for twelve years, though this need not mean that he was in residence throughout the period. In the first instance, his stay was a matter of months, rather than years (Neh. 2:6). After completing the re-building of the wall in fifty-two days, and dedicating it, Nehemiah gave the charge of the city into the hands of Hanani his brother and Hananiah the governor of the castle (7:2), as though himself about to return to Artaxerxes. It was on a second visit made in 432 that the reforms mentioned in Neh. 13 were carried out. Nehemiah's first action, after his arrival in 444, was to inspect the state of the wall, particularly on the southern and eastern sides where the damage was greatest. The Jewish community at this time seems to have been a rather loose union of groups held together by social or national ties, all living in a relatively small area around the city. The work was divided into forty-two portions, to be undertaken by different groups of people. Some were trade-guilds, the goldsmiths and perfumers; some

---

[1] Cowley, *Aramaic Papyri*, xxx, 18, xxxi, 17.
[2] 'Son' in Ezra 10:6 means 'grandson' as in Gen. 29:5.
[3] According to the useful note in H. H. Rowley, *Darius the Mede*, p. 49, this view was first suggested tentatively by Vernes.

were local groups, such as those of Tekoa; some were classes in the community, such as the priests. Six towns and nine districts seem to be represented. Notwithstanding both internal and external difficulties, the work was successfully completed in fifty-two days.

The external opposition was headed by Sanballat, the governor of Samaria. He would naturally be jealous of the rise of a neighbouring district to power and influence. He had support from others of the surrounding peoples, viz., the Arab tribes, the Ammonites and the Ashdodites (Philistines). He began with ridicule, but then threatened armed attack, under the old pretext that the building of the walls was an act of treason to the Persian king. Nehemiah effectively countered by arming his builders. There was no armed attack, but constant plotting went on; it is evident that Nehemiah had to face dissension in his own ranks, and that there was an influential party within the city consisting of those willing to build walls, but not to antagonize their neighbours, to whom some of them were bound by marriage ties (6:17–19). Sanballat proposed a discussion outside the city, hoping to seize the person of the governor; when this proposal was rejected, he bribed prophets within the city to mislead him.

Nehemiah, however, had other difficulties besides those created by the secret friends of Sanballat. The social and economic conditions were unfavourable. Prevalent poverty had been exploited by the wealthier classes, who foreclosed mortgages on land and houses and took Jewish children as slaves in payment of debts. Jewish law allowed the latter practice (Ex. 21:7–11; Dt. 15:12–18); the hardship was the exploitation of the hard times. Moreover, interest on loans was being taken, which was, in theory at least, forbidden (Ex. 22:25; Dt. 23:19, 20; 24:10–13). The governor himself had taken interest on loans, but stopped doing this when he saw the unprincipled lengths to which money-lenders were going. He was specially angry because some were trading in those Jewish slaves whom he and others were buying up in order to release them. (He himself did not draw the usual governor's salary, and provided generous hospitality.) Nehemiah took action by an open charge against the wealthier classes, and by the exaction from them of a solemn oath to release the real estate held, and to exact no future interest on loans. After the completion of the walls, Nehemiah had to take measures to re-populate the city. The community was a scattered agricultural one, to which the advantages (in time of peace) of living in a large, ruinous and thinly populated city would not be very evident. Only the leaders seem to have been living in Jerusalem (11:1). Accordingly, after a general assembly (7:4, 5), it was agreed to make an enforced draft of ten per cent of the whole population to provide settlers in Jerusalem, together with those who volunteered to join them (11:1 ff., the proper sequel).

The reforms carried out on Nehemiah's second visit (432) began with the expulsion of his old enemy Tobiah (possibly the governor of Ammon) from the temple-chamber, which he had been allowed to occupy through marriage-alliance with the high-priest, Eliashib. With characteristic energy, Nehemiah had the property of Tobiah thrown out of the room, and after cleansing the room from ceremonial pollution restored it to its proper and original use. The incident shows exactly the kind of vested interest against which any reformer would have to contend. Nehemiah then made proper provision for the Levites, whose tithes had been unpaid. Further, he stopped the Sabbath-trading which was being carried on, by closing the gates on that day, and by driving off all would-be traders from the vicinity. He was especially shocked by the prevalence of the marriages of Jews with women from the surrounding peoples, with the result that their children, learning their vernacular from their mothers, were ceasing to speak Hebrew. Even the grandson of the high-priest, Eliashib, had married San-ballat's daughter; him Nehemiah expelled from the city.

It seems probable that we must also credit Nehemiah with the 'covenant' made in Neh. 10, though the two preceding chapters (Neh. 8 and 9) belong to the Ezra-memoirs (worked over by the Chronicler).[1] He had already bound over the people to accept earlier reforms (Neh. 5:12, 13), and the terms of the present covenant show points of contact with some of the reforms mentioned in his own memoirs (13). Three commandments of the law of Moses (10:29) are accepted as basal, viz., no foreign marriages (Dt. 7:3), no Sabbath trading (Ex. 23:12, from the early Book of the Covenant), and the observance of the moratorium in the seventh year (Dt. 15:1; Ex. 23:11). All these, it will be noted, are sufficiently explained from the Book of the Covenant and Deuteronomy, long familiar to Israel. But from this point (Neh. 10:32) certain ordinances are accepted as if for the first time, viz., the provision of the wood-offering (cf. Neh. 13:31), for which there is no law in the Pentateuch, the poll-tax of a yearly third of a shekel for the upkeep of the Temple, whereas in the Priestly Code (Ex. 30:11–16) a half-shekel is exacted on a quite different basis, the offering of first-fruits, which is required in all the codes, the offering of the first-born, also a permanent item, and the tithes, which are claimed in both Deuteronomy and the Priestly Code. In these *ad hoc* ordinances, therefore, we seem to see legislation in the process of its creation, without any enforcement of an existent code. We can explain the covenant on the two-fold basis of earlier law and of contemporary needs, without any resort to the Priestly Code.

According to what has already been said, Ezra received his commission from the second Artaxerxes in 397 (Ezra 7:7); it was 'to inquire concerning Judah and Jerusalem, according to the law of thy God which is in thine hand' (*v.* 14). The further terms of the commission are doubtless paraphrased from a Jewish standpoint, but there need be no doubt as to the commission itself, as a measure for better local government, perhaps instigated by the stricter Judaism of Babylonia. The doubt is as to the extent of the 'law' which Ezra

[1] Cf. Eissfeldt, *Einleitung in das Alte Testament*, 2nd Ed. 1956, pp. 678 ff.

brought with him, and read solemnly to the people (Neh. 8). The people were moved to tears, as by something hitherto unknown to them. The observance of the Feast of Tabernacles which they obediently celebrated (8:14–18), agrees with the Law of Holiness (Lev. 23:39, 42) both as to manner (the dwelling in booths) and extent (the extra eighth day). The probability therefore is that Ezra's law-book was the Priestly Code (or such part of it as had already been elaborated in Babylon).[1] The subsequent addition of this code as a formally accepted law of God to the previously existent codes and the treasured stories of the patriarchs supplied the chief content of the Pentateuch, which was eventually to be the basis of Judaism.

Judaism as an exclusive community was thus the work of Nehemiah and Ezra. Politically, the community was wholly dependent on the Persian government, and was ruled by a Persian officer, who might be a Jew, as was Nehemiah. The Messianic hope lost its political character; we have no further identification of a particular individual, like Zerubbabel, with the Messianic prince until much later in the history; the eschatological side of the hope was developed, which made everything depend on God. A more individualized piety fed itself upon the religious literature of the past, and found its own literary expression, e.g., in many Psalms. In the absence of native rulers, the priests came into greater prominence. The observance of circumcision and the Sabbath and the cult became foremost religious duties. The closer identification of nationalism and religion undoubtedly helped the survival of Judaism through the trials which were eventually to come. Judaism might be stamped out by sheer force, but it was no longer in danger of absorption into other and lower forms of religion. If its quality and achievement seem far from being the realization of the higher prophetic hopes and ideals, yet the compromise of Judaism had its own

[1] I am not convinced by L. E. Browne's argument in *Early Judaism*, ch. X, that it was Deuteronomy. Still less is it likely to have been the whole Pentateuch, as is often assumed.

I

value; within the hard shell of the exclusive community, the kernel of prophetic aims to some extent found protection. How much difference this made to the Jews may be seen from the history of the rival community of Samaria.

3. THE SAMARITANS

The Samaritan schism was a result of the exclusive policy of Nehemiah and Ezra, though, like most schismatics, the Samaritans had a prior history of their own. They were the descendants of the old northern Israelites, and the semi-Baalized religion of their ancestors is portrayed for us through the contemporary prophecies of Amos and Hosea. Deportation and re-colonization after the fall of Samaria in 722 (see p. 71) doubtless favoured the introduction of foreign cults and the further degradation of the earlier Yahwism. In 621, Josiah carried the Deuteronomic reforms into Samaria (2 Kings 23:15–20), of which he had acquired temporary control, owing to the growing weakness of Assyria, of which it was a province. After the fall of Jerusalem in 586, we hear of pilgrims from Samaria going to worship at the ruined Temple (Jer. 41:5). This indication of continued religious dependence on Yahweh and His cult in the Temple at Jerusalem enables us better to understand the claims of the Samaritans to share in the restoration of the city under Nehemiah, and also helps us to understand why these claims had so much sympathy from within the city and from its priesthood. The ranks of these genuine worshippers of Yahweh were increased by the expulsion from Jerusalem of those who would not accept the measures of Nehemiah and Ezra. The most significant fact of all is that when the Samaritans do emerge as a distinct and rival community to Judaism, it is on the basis of the completed Pentateuch. They are thus more truly described as an arrested development of Judaism, than a continuance of the older religion of Israel, which is better represented by the Elephantine colony (see the next section).

It is unfortunate that we do not know the exact date of

the schism, which would have afforded a fixed point in the
history of the Canon. We saw that Nehemiah expelled a
grandson of the high priest, who had married a daughter of
the Samaritan governor, Sanballat. Long afterwards, Josephus
writes[1] that his name was Manasseh and his wife's name
Nicaso, and that Sanballat compensated his son-in-law for
the loss of his priestly inheritance in Jerusalem by building
for him a rival temple on Mount Gerizim, of which Manasseh
became the first high priest. Josephus, however, refers this
event to the time of Alexander the Great, a century after
Nehemiah. The Gerizim temple was probably built some
time in the fourth century, but even this would not fully
explain the ultimate religious division, which turns chiefly
on the claim that Gerizim and not Zion was the divinely
appointed place of worship.[2] The Elephantine colonists
appealed in 408-7 to both Jerusalem and the sons of Sanballat, which suggests that there was then no sharp cleavage
between the two communities. On the other hand, the
Chronicler indirectly reflects the *third* century attitude of the
Jews to the Samaritans, in his references to the northern
kingdom.[3] About 180 B.C., ben Sira refers to 'that foolish
people that dwelleth in Shechem' (50:26). Finally, John
Hyrcanus in 108 captured and destroyed Samaria, incor-
porating the district in the Maccabean territory. In spite of
some transient revivals, as in the fourth century A.D. (under
the leader, Baba Rabba and the theologian, Marqah), the
history of the Samaritans down to the now surviving handful
is significant for us chiefly as a 'control'. It shows us what
the post-exilic Judaism might have become without the
larger outlook and enthusiasm of the Pharisees, just as the
history of Moab shows us something of what the pre-exilic
Israel would have been without its prophets, from Moses
onwards.

[1] *Antiquities*, XI, vii, 2 and viii, 2 f.
[2] Cf. G. F. Moore, *Judaism*, I, p. 23 ff.; Oesterley, *History of Israel*,
p. 157.
[3] 2 Chron. 13:9; cf. 25:7: 'Yahweh is not with Israel.'

4. THE ELEPHANTINE COLONY

Early in the present century there were found a number of Aramaic papyri in the island of Elephantine, once a southern frontier-fortress of Egypt, close to the First Cataract. These reveal the existence of a Jewish settlement, dating back at least to the sixth century, since it was there in 525, when Cambyses conquered Egypt. Its origin seems to have been due to the employment of Jewish soldiers in Egypt, of which there is some indication even in the Book of Deuteronomy (17:16), i.e., in the seventh century. There is an explicit statement that Jewish troops were sent as auxiliaries to Psammeticus (probably the second of that name, 594–588).[1] These Jews had a fairly elaborate temple, and worshipped Yahu (Yahweh), though they felt no difficulty in making him share his offerings with other gods (Asham-bethel) and goddesses (Anath-bethel).[2] In 410, their temple, which Cambyses had spared more than a century before, was destroyed by Egyptian rebels against the Persian rule. Accordingly, they asked for permission to rebuild, and wrote to the governor of Judah and the high priest of Jerusalem to solicit their influence. To their first appeal in 410 no answer had been sent, so they wrote again in 407 to the governor of Judah and the sons of the governor of Samaria, and received a favourable reply. A papyrus of earlier date (419) reports Persian orders to the Persian governor of the Elephantine settlement for the celebration of the Passover,[3] forming an interesting parallel to the Persian interest in, and approval of, the work of Nehemiah and Ezra.

The papyri have considerable historical value, especially as they are dated. Bagohi, the governor of Judah, is the Bagoses of whom Josephus writes[4] that he intervened in the affairs of the Jerusalem Temple, when his protégé, Jesus, was killed by his own brother, John (Jehochanan) the high priest, c. 400. The name of the high priest, Jehochanan, as

[1] *Epistle of Aristeas*, 13.
[2] Cowley, *Aramaic Papyri*, p. 72.
[3] *Ibid.*, p. 63.
[4] *Antiquities*, XI, vii.

we have already seen, helps us to date Ezra's work, as does the reference to the sons of Sanballat, Delaiah and Shemaiah, who appear to have been his deputies or successors. Of particular interest is the association of Yahweh with other deities, including the goddess Anath. This and other features suggest that we have here an echo of Israelite religion in Palestine, prior to the reformation of Josiah, of which these Jews show no knowledge.[1] The papyri serve to remind us that the Yahwism which runs through a great part of the Old Testament is by no means that purified and monotheistic form of religion which ultimately prevailed. In particular, we notice the sexual element of Semitic religion associated with Yahweh through the goddess Anath, his consort. In the light of these documents, we can better realize what it was the prophets were opposing, and the greatness of their contribution.

5. THE PERSIAN BACKGROUND

We have already noticed how the fortunes of the Jews were affected by the conquests of Cyrus (550–529), ushering in the Persian Empire. His successor, Cambyses (529–522), is chiefly notable for his conquest of Egypt. After a period of great disorder (521–518), Darius I (Hystaspis) established himself. He is remembered for his masterly organization of the empire into twenty satrapies, Syria and Palestine being included in that of Arabia. By making the satrap a purely civil governor, and keeping the military forces under direct imperial control, Darius did much to promote peace and order. 'Like the Roman Empire later, the great means of control and unity was the road system, with its posting-houses and state-couriers. The spread of a uniform coinage throughout the empire, giving a fixed standard of exchange, was another help to intercourse. . . . The care for health was far advanced. At a time when the Greek reached the

---

[1] A. Vincent, *La Religion des Judéo-Araméens d'Elephantine*, argues that the colony continued the semi-pagan worship of Yahweh at *Bethel*, the migration being due to Josiah's reforming activities there.

improvement of a ledge in his drinking-cup to keep back the grit, the Persian was boiling all the water-supply of the court in silver cauldrons when on campaign.'[1]

Both Darius I (521–485) and Xerxes (485–464) cherished the purpose to conquer Greece, with which are linked the undying names of Marathon (490), Thermopylae and Salamis (480) and Plataea (479). Xerxes is the Ahasuerus of the quite unhistorical romance known as the Book of Esther. Artaxerxes I (464–425) was the patron of Nehemiah; we have seen his (characteristic) change of policy in regard to Jerusalem, dictated by personal favouritism. From his reign and that of his successor,[2] Darius II (424–405), there are hundreds of cuneiform tablets relating to the business affairs of Murashu Sons in Nippur, which throw light on the condition of the Jews in Babylonia.[3] Many of them were prosperous agriculturists, others held official posts, some were engaged in trade. We can understand from this glimpse of them why many were able to send contributions to their so much poorer brethren in Judaea, such as that of which we hear as early as the time of the re-building of the Temple.[4]

Artaxerxes II (404–358) by whom Ezra was commissioned to go to Jerusalem, is linked to world-history by the rebellion of his younger brother Cyrus, and the connected 'Anabasis' of Xenophon (400 B.C.), a story which reveals the growing weakness of the Persian Empire. His successor, Artaxerxes III (Ochus, 358–338), figures obscurely in Jewish history through two brief and enigmatic references in ancient chronicles.[5] He had to deal with revolts in the western part of his empire, including Palestine, in which the Jews seem to have shared. He is said to have deported some of them to Hyrcania, near the Caspian Sea, whilst both Jerusalem and Jericho were taken and destroyed. We have no corroboration or amplifica-

[1] Flinders Petrie, *Eastern Exploration*, pp. 44–5.
[2] Xerxes II reigned for a few months only.
[3] Lods, *The Prophets and the Rise of Judaism*, p. 195.
[4] Zech. 6: 9 ff.
[5] The documents are conveniently quoted in L. E. Browne, *Early Judaism*, pp. 202–3.

tion of these scanty statements, though it is known that Sidon, the head of the Phoenician revolt, was so hard pressed by the mercenaries of Ochus that the inhabitants set fire to their own fleet and city, and large numbers perished. The date of this Jewish deportation given in the Chronicle of Eusebius is 353.

The last of the Persian kings was Darius III (Codomannus, 338–331). He was called to an impossible task, that of facing the might of Alexander the Great, and the Persian Empire came to an end with the battles of the River Granicus (334), the pass of Issus (333) and Gaugamela (331).

The two centuries of Persian rule were of the greatest importance in the history of Judaism. This is not because of any direct influence on the religion which can be traced to Zoroastrianism, and may be seen in particular in Jewish apocalyptic and angelology. Such influences are still largely matter of debate, and the debate is complicated by the blending of so many elements, Babylonian and Iranian and Egyptian and Greek, in the culture and civilization of the times. The importance is that the patronage of the Persian Empire enabled the religious passion nurtured through the exile to find an effective outlet in the re-establishment of the Temple and its cult. Around this centre, it was possible for Judaism to develop without political interference. The great religious ideas which history had created could now be articulated and applied in an age which had little history to record. It was the opportunity for development and consolidation provided by the Persian peace which prepared the Jews for the battles which were to face them in the Greek period.

VIII.—THE JEWS IN THE GREEK PERIOD
(333–63 B.C.)

1. THE PTOLEMIES AND THE SELEUCIDS

PHILIP of Macedon, the father of Alexander the Great, having skilfully acquired both real and titular supremacy in the Hellenic Confederacy, was planning an invasion of the Persian Empire, the hereditary enemy of the Greeks, when he was assassinated in 336. His son, inspired by far-reaching ambitions, found himself at the head of a small, but highly efficient army and flung himself into his father's project with the enthusiasm of youth—he was scarcely twenty—and with the genius of a born commander. Early in 334, he crossed the Hellespont and won a battle near the River Granicus, which made him master of Asia Minor. His next victory was at the pass of Issus (near the angle made by the coasts of Asia Minor and Syria) in 333. He did not pursue the fugitive Darius III, but turned south to Phoenicia, which he overran, though he had to besiege Tyre for seven months; his conquest of Phoenician seaports deprived the Persians of their fleet. He captured Gaza after two months' siege, passed on to Egypt, where he was welcomed, and founded the future city of Alexandria. His third decisive victory was that won at Gaugamela, east of Nineveh, when the Persian Empire came to an end. It is not necessary to follow his further progress into the East, or the plans for a vast empire, which were shattered by his death in 323. He seems to have left the occupation of Palestine to his general Parmenio; probably the Jews passed quietly from the Persian to the Greek over-lord, though Samaria offered some resistance.

The germ of historical truth in the picturesque legend[1] of Alexander's reception at Jerusalem by the high priest is that the Jews were allowed to continue their home-rule in religious matters; possibly also there was some adjustment of disputed territory held by Samaria.[2]

The death of Alexander was followed by protracted strife amongst his generals, from which three kingdoms were evolved. One was that of the former Macedonia, which does not concern us; the others were Egypt and the large and rather vaguely defined territory which formed the kingdom of the Seleucids (so called after Seleucus I, 312–280). Though Egypt was the smaller, it was more compact and more easily to be defended. Ptolemy, its governor, secured Palestine by his victory at Gaza in 312, and Palestine remained more or less under the control of Egypt until 198, when it passed to the Seleucid kingdom, which had the Syrian Antioch as one of its capital centres. Ptolemy occupied Jerusalem, entering it on a Sabbath, as though about to offer sacrifice[3]; he transplanted many thousands of Jews to Egypt, partly captives from Judaea and Samaria, and partly volunteers. He gave equal privileges of citizenship to these Jews with his own Macedonians in Alexandria. Privileges were also given to the Jews in Antioch by Seleucus I, who began the Seleucid dynasty there, after conquering Babylon, in 312. Thenceforward, the political fortunes of the Jews were to depend on these two kingdoms to the west and to the east, just as in the ancient days—since history always goes back to geography for some of its chief *motifs*. The difference from the ancient days, however, lay in the fact that both these kingdoms, the Ptolemaic and the Seleucid, shared in the common Hellenistic culture and civilization, which had been so widely spread by the victories of Alexander. The influence of this culture continued through all the rivalries and strife of Ptolemy and Seleucid, and little difference in this respect was made by one

---

[1] Josephus, *Antiquities*, XI, viii.
[2] *contra Apionem*, II, 4.
[3] *Antiquities*, XII, i.

or the other getting the upper hand. This culture[1] centred in the city state, modelled on that of Greece; most of the cities in the nearer East were 'Hellenized' more or less after this pattern. The outer signs of the change were the gymnasium, the stadium and the hippodrome, with their athletic sports, the theatre, with its performance of Greek drama, the senate-hall for the city council, the fashionable Greek dress, the public eating-halls, and the many festivals. The inner signs of the change would be those that sprang from a naturalistic religion with many images and cults, a general loosening of morality, and a good deal of vice. We must not think of these things as remote from the areas of Jewish life; there were Greek cities all through Palestine, and no Jew could easily avoid contact with this culture. We can understand the force of the remark made by a writer in the first half of the third century: 'In recent times, under the foreign rule of the Persians, and then of the Macedonians, by whom the Persian Empire was overthrown, intercourse with other races has led to many of the traditional Jewish ordinances losing their hold.'[2]

At some time during this century, and according to tradition, under the second Ptolemy (Philadelphus, 285–247), the Hebrew 'Torah' (our Pentateuch) was translated into Greek, for the benefit of those Greek-speaking Jews in Egypt who had ceased to understand Hebrew. (In Palestine itself, and for the same reason, it became customary for the Hebrew Scripture lessons to be translated—for a long time only orally—into the vernacular Aramaic.) The name of the Greek version, subsequently extended from the 'Law' to other parts of the Old Testament, is the 'Septuagint'; this is derived from the story[3] that seventy (properly seventy-two)

---

[1] The best description is that in E. Bevan's *Jerusalem under the High-Priests*, pp. 34 ff.; see also D. G. Hogarth, *The Ancient East*, pp. 224 ff.

[2] Hecataeus of Abdera, as cited by Bevan, *op. cit.*, p. 43.

[3] This story, with many legendary accretions, comes to us from a document known as 'The Epistle of Aristeas', on which Josephus is wholly dependent. A critical examination of it is given by H. B. Swete, *Introduction to the Old Testament in Greek*, Chap. I.

chosen elders of Israel had made it, at the request of Ptolemy
Philadelphus, prompted by his librarian, Demetrius Phale-
reus. The importance of this Greek Bible for the wider
Judaism of the Dispersion can hardly be overrated. It served
to maintain and educate the widespread Judaism of the
Roman world, and was the essential basis for that Jewish
propaganda which resulted in so remarkable an extension of
Judaism. From this point onwards, and indeed from an
earlier point, as Jer. 40–44 and the Elephantine papyri show,
we have to think of a Judaism of the western Dispersion as
well as of the Judaism of Babylonia. This Diaspora became
far greater in numbers than the Judaism of Palestine, though
the latter naturally retained its central place. It is, perhaps,
significant that our first dated evidence for the existence of
the synagogues (which probably originated in the necessities
of the Babylonian exile) comes from Egypt, and from the
century which saw the Law translated into Greek.[1] The
synagogue was primarily the place for the study of the Law,
as distinct from the Temple as the place of sacrifice, though
each naturally developed the praise and prayer of worship
around its characteristic nucleus. Eventually the synagogue
consciously provided a spiritual sacrifice to replace the
material sacrifice of the Temple. By that time, however, the
Greek Bible had passed into the possession of the Christian
Church—it was the Bible of the New Testament writers.
Hellenistic Judaism gradually disappeared and the rest of the
Jews were left with their Hebrew Scriptures and their
Aramaic Targums.

As to the central Judaism of Palestine, we have valuable
evidence in the Biblical book of 'Chronicles', which sub-
stantially belongs to the third century B.C. However un-
reliable its handling of the earlier history, the very way in
which this is done shows us the world in which the writer or
writers lived. The people are still the people of a cult, which,
with its related institutions, is supposed to have been the
same in ancient times as in those of the Chronicles. (The

[1] Elbogen, *Der Jüdische Gottesdienst*,³, pp. 446–7.

change of emphasis to the 'Law', already visible in a few Psalms, had not yet taken place.) The Temple, with all its ecclesiastical officers, is in the centre of the picture. The priests are divided into twenty-four classes (1 Chron. 24), as are also the Levites (23:3–32; 24:20–31)—new features since the days of Nehemiah and Ezra. The temple-singers, not named in the Pentateuch, but classed in the Ezra–Nehemiah sources next *after* the Levites (Neh. 7:44; 11:23; 12:28), are in Chronicles reckoned *among* the Levites (1 Chron. 23:5); they have risen in the ecclesiastical world, and they also are divided into twenty-four classes. The door-keepers also (next after the singers under Nehemiah) are now included, in much larger numbers, among the Levites (1 Chron. 23:4). The ecclesiastical organization and the music of the Temple are ascribed to David (1 Chron. 23:1–6), in accordance with the doubtless contemporary ascription of many of the Psalms to him. The whole reconstruction of the history according to the pattern of third-century beliefs and practices is valuable as showing that Israel's religion was necessarily embedded in history, and had to be justified by it. A contributory picture of the Temple ritual, about a century after the Chronicler's time, is that of ben Sira (ch. 50), who describes in enthusiastic terms the ritual in the time of Simon the high priest.

We must not think, however, that contemporary Judaism was wholly of this ideal pattern. Its darker side is revealed in the full-length portraits of a certain Joseph and of his son, Hyrcanus, which Josephus supplies.[1] In the second half of the century the high-priest was Onias II, 'one of a little soul and a great lover of money', as Josephus says, with the pen of a Tacitus. Onias was responsible for the annual tribute of twenty talents of silver to Egypt, but withheld payment. His nephew, Joseph, offered to act as ambassador to Ptolemy (Euergetes, 247–222). By shrewd diplomacy and lavish bribery, he won favour with Ptolemy and Cleopatra, and secured control of the ingathering of taxes in Palestine,

[1] *Antiquities*, XII, iv.

backed by a military force. By pitiless and unscrupulous measures, he maintained himself in this position for twenty-two years. His son Hyrcanus, who followed in his father's footsteps, was the issue of a most disgraceful amour. Hyrcanus kept royal state in a fortress beyond the Jordan for seven years, until he committed suicide on being threatened with attack by Antiochus Epiphanes. The comment of Josephus on the career of Joseph is: 'He was a good man, and of great magnanimity, and brought the Jews out of a state of poverty and meanness to one that was more splendid' —a comment which throws some light on Josephus himself. The baleful legacy of the family (known as the Tobiadae, from the name of the father of Joseph) was that a feud between Hyrcanus and other members of it divided the people, and contributed to the disorders which were to occasion Seleucid intervention.

The transference of Palestine from the control of the Ptolemies to that of the Seleucids occurred in the time of Antiochus the Great (223–187). He is 'the king of the north' mentioned in Dan. 11 (v. 12), who 'shall cast down tens of thousands, but shall not prevail'. This refers to his defeat of the Egyptians in 218, and his own severe defeat by them at Raphia in 217. The 'well-fenced city' of v. 15 is Sidon, captured by Antiochus in 198. This year marked the downfall of Egyptian power in Palestine (v. 16), and Antiochus now 'stands in the glorious land', threatening Egypt. The plans of Antiochus in Asia Minor brought him up against the Romans, who defeated him at Magnesia in 190 (v. 18). This was followed by his withdrawal to his own territory, and his death through the people of a Persian town, which he had plundered to pay the Roman indemnities (v. 19). He is said to have been welcomed by the Jews of Jerusalem,[1] and to have made certain concessions to them. He made another contribution to the Diaspora by transporting Jews from Babylon to Asia Minor. Of the general condition of the inhabitants of Palestine, including Judaea, during the period

[1] Josephus, *Antiquities*, XII, iii, 3.

of Antiochus, Josephus remarks that they 'were equally sufferers, both when he was beaten and when he beat the others: so that they were very like to a ship in a storm, which is tossed by the waves on both sides'.[1]

It was in the times of Antiochus that there arose a strife about the priesthood, significant in itself, and having important consequences. Onias III, who had succeeded Simon II as the last of the legitimate high priests, had for rival his own brother Jason (Jesus); the latter became high priest for a time, and was then displaced by Menelaus, a change which led to further disorder, in which the Tobiadae were involved:

'The sons of Tobias took the part of Menelaus, but the greater part of the people assisted Jason; and by that means Menelaus and the sons of Tobias were distressed, and retired to Antiochus, and informed him that they were desirous to leave the laws of their country and the Jewish way of living according to them, and to follow the king's laws, and the Grecian way of living: wherefore they desired his permission to build them a gymnasium at Jerusalem.'

(Josephus, *Antiquities*, XII, v, 1; Whiston's trans.)

The Antiochus here named is not Antiochus the Great, but Antiochus Epiphanes; in this party of Jewish Hellenizers we see signs of the crisis which was the cause of the Maccabean revolt.

2. THE MACCABEES

It was in 175 that Antiochus Epiphanes began the reign[2] which was to make acute the issue between Judaism and Hellenism. He was a ruler of remarkable personality. Dr. Edwyn Bevan[3] has characterized him as possessing an ardent imagination, to which Hellenism appealed, an impul-

---

[1] Whiston's translation, *loc. cit.*

[2] He had to overthrow Heliodorus, who had murdered Seleucus IV, the brother of Antiochus. It was this Heliodorus who, as the prime minister of Seleucus, attempted to confiscate the Temple treasures (2 Macc. 3, cf. Dan. 11:20).

[3] *Op. cit.*, pp. 74–6.

sive and high-spirited temperament, combined with a strong
grasp of affairs and a talent for diplomacy, whilst there was
perhaps a touch of insanity in this curiously complex king.[1]
The peaceful penetration of Judaism by Hellenism, which
had been going on for generations, was now to be replaced by
a more active policy—that of unifying the Seleucid kingdom
on the basis of Hellenic culture and religion, each city being
given a large measure of local freedom. With all other states
this policy seems to have been successful, and Judaism is said
to be the only example of an Oriental religion completely
emancipating itself from the influence of Hellenism.[2] This
was because the Hellenizers were faced by the Hasidim, the
predecessors of the Pharisees, and their spirit, though not
their political quietism, inspired an heroic fighting resistance
to persecution. The occasion for this was that struggle for the
high-priesthood which was mentioned at the close of the
previous section. In 169, Antiochus was carrying on a
campaign against Egypt. The false report of his death
prompted Jason, the dispossessed high-priest, to attack his
successful rival Menelaus. Antiochus, ordered by Rome in
the person of Popillius Laenas to abandon his designs on
Egypt, turned aside on his way back to chastise these
turbulent Jews. He took the opportunity to plunder the
Temple (1 Macc. 1:21, 22), and seems now to have decided
on his more active measures against the Jewish faith. He
erected an altar to the Olympian Zeus (apparently with an
image) on the altar of burnt-offerings in the court of the
Temple.[3] This was the 'abomination which desolates',[4] the
focus of offence in Jewish eyes. This event of 168 was
followed by the bitter and cruel persecution of those Jews

---

[1] Cf. Polybius, *Histories*, XXXI, 11.

[2] Schürer, *Geschichte des Jüdischen Volkes*, Erster Theil, §4; Eng.
trans., *The Jewish People in the Time of Christ*, Div. I, Vol. I, p. 199.

[3] 1 Macc. 1:54; Dan. 11:31, on which see Driver's note.

[4] This is the proper meaning of the conventional 'Abomination of
desolation', so often misunderstood; the Hebrew participle is active, and
denotes that which desolates, or rather 'appals'. The Hebrew (*shiqquṣ
meshomem*) appears to be a play on the title of the god, viz., *ba'al
shamayim*.

who remained faithful to the Law; to this period belong the partly legendary stories of martyrdom recounted in 2 Maccabees.[1]

The persecution met at first with only passive resistance, and one narrative describes the slaughter of a thousand men, women and children on a Sabbath, when they would do nothing to profane it (1 Macc. 2:29–38). But there was also an active patriotism, waiting only to be aroused. The stimulus came from the village of Modein, a few miles east of Lydda. Here lived a priest called Mattathias, with his five sons. When the officer of Antiochus came to Modein to enforce heathen sacrifice, Mattathias not only refused to obey, but was enraged to the point of killing a renegade Jew who did sacrifice, together with the king's officer. Mattathias and his sons, fugitives because of this deed, speedily became the nucleus of a fighting force, which made the mountains their base for an offensive against all Hellenizers. They were joined by the Hasidim, who had realized that a merely passive resistance meant suicide. The accession of the Hasidim to the guerilla band of Mattathias was of great importance, for it gave full religious sanction to the revolt. The rebels 'went round about and pulled down the altars; and they circumcised by force the children that were uncircumcised' (1 Macc. 2:45, 46). These local tactics marked the first phase of the Maccabean rebellion. When Mattathias died in 166, he nominated his third son Judas as captain of the band, and Judas was successful in defeating such royal forces as were sent against him. The Book of Daniel, written in the following year, makes curiously slight reference to the Maccabean rising, but this is to be explained by the fact that the revolt had not yet gone much beyond the stage of guerilla fighting, as well as by the supreme emphasis of the book on the eschatological and supernatural side of things, which threw all human agencies into the shade. Thus the Hasidim, to whom the author of Daniel belonged, were much more

---

[1] Cf. 6 and 7 (Eleazar and the seven brothers with their mother); cf. 4 Macc. 5 ff.

important in his eyes than Judas and his followers, whose work is but 'a little help'[1] in comparison with that which was about to come, the great help of the appointed time, when the archangel Michael should usher in the day of deliverance.

The Maccabean revolt passed out of the stage of guerilla fighting into something like a national struggle when the regent Lysias came into the field with a new commission from Antiochus. It was no longer a question of the enforced Hellenization of the Jews, but of the destruction of their nationality and the recolonization of their land; it is significant that slave-dealers accompanied the Seleucid forces.[2] In 165, Lysias advanced against Judas from the less protected south, through Idumaea. The engagement at Beth-zur is claimed as a victory for Judas; at any rate, he was left free to occupy Jerusalem (except the fortress known as the Acra) and to reconsecrate the Temple (December 165; three years after its desecration).[3] He further consolidated his position by campaigns against hostile neighbours and by bringing in the scattered Jews from Gilead and Galilee. His attack on the Acra in 163 (after the death of Antiochus) brought another Syrian army against him, which defeated him at the battle of Beth-zecharias, where his brother Eleazar died a hero's death. Jerusalem was besieged and hard pressed, but the appearance of another claimant to the Seleucid throne compelled Lysias[4] to make terms with Judas, leaving him with dismantled defences, but with the full restoration of religious liberty. Thus, the year 162 draws a definite line in the history of the struggle; the aim of the Hasidim was reached, and the Maccabean party, still eager for political freedom, were deprived of their support. This may be seen in the welcome they gave to Alcimus, who was appointed high-priest by Demetrius (the successor

---

[1] Dan. 11:33–5; cf. 12:1 ff.
[2] 1 Macc. 3:41, referring to the earlier operations.
[3] 1 Macc. 4:36 ff.
[4] Now acting in the name of the youthful son of Antiochus.

K

to Antiochus V and Lysias, whom he had killed). Alcimus was recognized by the Hasidim as a legitimate Aaronite priest, though the welcome must have been cooled through the slaughter of sixty of them by the troops which came to instal him. Alcimus, however, had to appeal to Demetrius for further help, and Nicanor arrived to attack Judas, but was defeated and slain at Adasa ('Nicanor's Day'). When, however, a further Syrian army came, Judas was deserted by many of his followers and was defeated and killed at Elasa (160). The change in the Jewish fortunes was due in part, no doubt, to the defection of the Hasidim, but still more to the fact that the Seleucid kingdom was now united under a strong ruler, who could concentrate his attention on the Jewish insurgents.

After the death of Judas, the fortunes of the insurgents were at a low ebb; they were forced back into the initial position of guerilla fighting. Jonathan, who succeeded his brother Judas in the command, eventually established himself at Michmash. After the death of Alcimus, the Syrian forces were withdrawn. It was not until 153 that a new phase was initiated by the rise of the usurper Alexander Balas, who claimed the throne from Demetrius, as being the son of Antiochus Epiphanes. Both the rivals saw that Jonathan and his supporters would be a valuable asset in the struggle, and both made overtures to him. Demetrius formally recognized his position, and handed over certain hostages who had been kept in the Acra, whilst Jonathan was now enabled to fortify Jerusalem. But Alexander Balas was able to outbid Demetrius, by making Jonathan high-priest, and bestowing other honours. As long as Alexander lived, Jonathan remained faithful to him; after his murder in 146, he transferred his support to Demetrius II. When the latter was driven out by Tryphon, acting on behalf of the son of Alexander Balas, Jonathan was confirmed in his high-priesthood, and his brother Simon was made governor of the coast. But Tryphon felt that Jonathan was in the way of his own designs to take the place of his ward, and by treachery he took Jonathan prisoner and eventually killed him (143).

Simon naturally took his brother's place, and successfully resisted the attacks of Tryphon. His work was to consolidate the gains and to confirm the independence won by the valiant struggle of Judas and the shrewd diplomacy of Jonathan. Demetrius II found it wise to recognize this independence (1 Macc. 13:34 ff.) and Simon strengthened it by reducing the two important fortresses still holding out against him, Gazara on the great coast road and the Acra at Jerusalem, which had been in the occupation of the Hellenizers for nearly forty years. The year 143–2 was that in which 'the people began to write in their instruments and contracts, "In the first year of Simon the great high-priest and captain and leader of the Jews"' (v. 42). A memorial of this recognition of Simon as high-priest is possibly to be found in Psalm 110, which celebrates the accession of a priest-prince. A more tangible evidence of Simon's establishment is in the coinage which he was permitted to strike, of which specimens are extant, though the famous monument to his family which he erected at Modein has long since perished. The decree of the people conferring on him the office of high-priest, forever (i.e., with hereditary rights) was engraven in bronze and set up in the Temple. He sent an embassy and offering to Rome, which were welcomed by the Romans.[1] The historian of the Maccabean rebellion, to whom we owe so much unique information, legitimately rises into a poetical strain as he celebrates the new-found peace of Simon's time, when once more, after these weary and harassing years, the old men could sit in the streets and the farmer could plough his land with a reasonable hope of reaping his harvest.

But Simon was not destined to end his days in peace, any more than had been Judas and Jonathan. A new Antiochus (VII) tried to exact heavy tribute from him as an alternative

[1] 1 Macc. 14:24, 15:15 ff. Judas also is reported to have sent to Rome (8), but Rome's first real recognition of the Jews seems to have been in Simon's time. See p. 140.

to the surrender of the strong cities. A Syrian army under Cendebaeus was sent against Simon, and he gave the Jewish military operations into the hands of his sons, Judas and John. There is dramatic fitness in the fact that they met the invader near to Modein. Near the spot where the Maccabean rebellion had first begun, through the passionate act of Mattathias, the last battle was fought. Where the priest Mattathias had slain the king's officer on a Syrian altar, his grandson, John, afterwards to be known as Hyrcanus, led the hesitating Jewish soldiers across a stream to put Cendebaeus to flight. It was less easy to banish the invasive passions of jealousy and ambition. Ptolemy, the son-in-law of Simon, and captain of the plain of Jericho, aimed at the supreme place in Judaea. He beguiled his father-in-law and his brother-in-law, Judas, into his castle, made them drunk and murdered them. He would have assassinated John Hyrcanus also at Gazara, but for a timely warning which enabled John to save himself, and so to succeed to his father's place.

It is perhaps suggestive to compare these three brothers who for a season raised their country to political independence with the three men who began the Hebrew monarchy. Both Saul and Judas were fighters, first and last, and both came to a tragic end, with their aims unaccomplished. David was a much greater man than Jonathan, yet both men laid a foundation for their successors, and both knew the art of diplomacy. Solomon and Simon both reaped where others had sown, consolidated and organized and enjoyed prosperity and left a line of ruling successors.

3. The Hasmonaeans

The name 'Hasmonaean' is used in Rabbinic literature for the Maccabees and their descendants, and is derived, according to Josephus, from the great-grandfather of Mattathias. But it is customary and convenient to keep the name 'Maccabee', belonging properly to Judas only, for the three brothers who combined to liberate the Jews from foreign dominion, and to use the name 'Hasmonaean' for those descendants of the Maccabees under whom the Jews enjoyed another seventy years of independence.

There are five of these to be considered. John Hyrcanus I succeeded his father Simon, who had been murdered by his son-in-law, Ptolemy, and ruled for thirty years, for the most part happily and prosperously. He was succeeded by his son Aristobulus I for a single year; Josephus accuses him of great cruelty, but the story may be due to Pharisaic dislike of his pro-Greek leanings, and there is external evidence that he was capable and useful to the Jews. His successor was a younger son of Hyrcanus, viz., Alexander Jannaeus, who reigned for twenty-six years, an ambitious and successful, but cruel and unpopular ruler. In him culminated the Jewish power of this period of independence. After him Alexandra, who had been the wife of both Aristobulus and Jannaeus, remained as queen for nine years of uneventful rule; her sagacity in the difficult situation caused by the strife of religious parties suggests comparison with our own Queen Elizabeth. With her death in 67 B.C. began the troubles which led to the intervention of Rome; her youngest son, Aristobulus II, became king, whilst her elder son, Hyrcanus, remained high-priest.

It will be remembered that the ancestor of the Hasmonaeans, Mattathias, was of priestly stock, and that the Jews in 143 had recognized Simon as high-priest, making the office hereditary two years afterwards. (Jonathan had been recognized as high-priest by the Syrians, but not formally by the Jews.) The evidence of the coinage is useful in showing the exact status of the Hasmonaeans. Hyrcanus struck a number of copper coins with the inscription 'Jehochanan the high-priest and the Senate of the Jews' showing that his authority was formally based on the decree of 141 (1 Macc. 14:28). Aristobulus used the same formula on his coins, though Josephus says that he was the first to call himself king; possibly this was in foreign relations. The coins of Jannaeus show a marked advance, by the use of the title 'king', as well as by the use of Greek as well as Hebrew characters; both features symbolize his alienation from his Jewish subjects. This secularization of the high-priesthood, as we shall see, was strongly resented by the Pharisees and their supporters. The period began unfavourably, for Hyrcanus was besieged in Jerusalem by the Syrians and had to come to terms with Antiochus VII, paying tribute and giving hostages. But the death of Antiochus gave Hyrcanus the opportunity of breaking loose and, in due course, of extending his territory. From that time the Jews were untroubled by the Seleucids; in fact, the Jewish opponents of Jannaeus actually invoked the help of Syria against their tyrannical king.

The relations with Rome deserve mention. In 161 Judas had appealed to Rome for help, and secured formal recognition, though it brought no direct help. Indeed, it might be said that the restraint set on Antiochus Epiphanes by the Romans had been one of the causes leading him to the Hellenization of his empire. Yet it also hindered him in the attempt to carry it out. Roman policy was unfavourable to the growth of Syrian power, and was responsible for some of the rival claimants who gave the Maccabees their opportunity (e.g., Balas). Jonathan (1 Macc. 12:1) is also said to have made overtures to Rome, which does appear to have recognized Simon (1 Macc. 14:16; 15:15 ff.), though it has been argued that such recognition really belongs to the time of Hyrcanus. It is disputed whether the appeal of Hyrcanus to Rome falls before or after the surrender of Jerusalem to Antiochus VII; on the whole it is more likely to have followed it, possibly in connection with the pressure of Demetrius, the successor of Antiochus, upon Hyrcanus. Josephus reports a decree of the Roman Senate, confirming Hyrcanus in his independence, and warning the Syrians against interfering with him. Otherwise, all that the Romans did was to pay the expenses of the Jewish embassy back to their homes. In fact, the Hasmonaeans were able to maintain themselves against Syria without help from Rome, owing to the growing weakness of Syria, harassed by the Parthians on the east, and undermined by Roman diplomacy. The Hasmonaean independence was secured from 129, when Antiochus was killed in a campaign against the Parthians, until the internal strife of the Jews led to the intervention of Pompey in 63.

The Extension of Territory. One of the important features of this Hasmonaean period is the growth of Jewish territory until the time of Jannaeus, who ultimately attained a kingdom almost as large as that of Solomon. The stages of this success should be noted. Hyrcanus used the opportunity given by the death of Antiochus to extend his territory in all directions. To the south, he incorporated Idumaea, and judaized the inhabitants by compelling them to be circumcised. To the north of Judaea, he seized Samaritan territory, destroying the rival temple on Mount Gerizim. He also pushed eastwards into Moab, capturing certain cities. The tribute which he had agreed to pay Antiochus for Joppa and other cities ceased with the death of Antiochus. In 109 the continued civil wars in Syria enabled him to attack the Greek city of Samaria itself, the Samaritans having given him the occasion by their attack on a colony he had planted. The Samaritans naturally appealed to Syria, but Syria's attempt to relieve the siege was unsuccessful. After a year the city was taken and utterly destroyed by the sons of Hyrcanus, whom he had left in charge of the siege-operations. The next step forward in the acquisition of territory was taken by the successor of Hyrcanus, viz., Aristobulus. He added a great part of Ituraea, which probably means Galilee. Hyrcanus had extended his rule to the line from Mount Carmel to Beth-shean, viz., the valley of Esdraelon; Aristobulus now added Galilee, and judaized the inhabitants as Hyrcanus had done those of Idumaea. In this district the Gentile element had outweighed the Jewish, and this continued to be true racially. This fact is important for the future history, since Galilee was destined to be the cradle of Christianity.

It was the ambition of Alexander Jannaeus to round off the Jewish kingdom, especially by conquering the Greek cities. He first attacked Ptolemais (Akko) with a view to getting control of the coast, but this attempt was defeated by Egyptian aid to the besieged, and Ptolemy, who had been expelled from Egypt by his mother Cleopatra, disastrously defeated Alexander and overran the country. Cleopatra came to Alexander's aid, being persuaded by one of her generals, Ananias, who was a Jew, not to try to annex Judaea. After a long struggle Alexander conquered most of the coast from Gaza to Carmel, though not Ashkelon, and not Ptolemais, north of Carmel. He also extended his territory both southwards and east of the Jordan, which brought him into contact with the Arabs. He was in fact engaged in one of these many campaigns to acquire isolated cities when he died. The territory of Alexander Jannaeus was maintained under his widow, Alexandra, without further extension; an expedition of his son Aristobulus against Damascus came to nothing. Alexandra maintained a large army of mercenaries. After her death began the civil strife which finally involved the loss of Jewish independence.

The Pharisees and the Sadducees. The most important, indeed, the ultimately dominating factor of the internal history of this period, is the conflict of those who eventually came to be known as the Pharisees and Sadducees; it is characteristic of the history of Israel throughout its course that the political and religious factors should thus be intermingled. Both parties go back for their origin to the time of the Maccabees, when we found the Hasidim (whom we might think of as the Church within the civil community), already distinct from the Maccabean fighters for national independence, though joining with them to gain religious liberty; political liberty was for the Hasidim a secondary matter. This religious group was continued through the subsequent generations in the Pharisees. Over against this 'churchly' party we have the 'worldly' party. This at first consisted of patriotic Jews using ordinary means of war and diplomacy to regain their political liberty; it was reinforced by the dependants and relatives of the Hasmonaean aristocracy, with their broader outlook on culture and life (note their Greek contacts), combined with a narrower and more conservative outlook in religion. Such a group stood in strong contrast with the religiously progressive Pharisees, who were now in their formative period, and had not yet reached the fixity of traditional belief displayed in the New Testament. The Pharisees became the religious leaders of the people, over against the new Sadducean aristocracy. Josephus, in his loose way, mentions the Pharisees (with the Sadducees and the Essenes) as in existence under Jonathan; but the first emergence of the Pharisees into definite history falls under Hyrcanus. The reason is that Hyrcanus carried further and to greater success the secular policy of Jonathan and Simon. The occasion[1] of the breach of the Pharisees with Hyrcanus was trifling, as often happens with great issues. Hyrcanus seems to have invited the Pharisees, whom he was entertaining at a banquet, to criticize his general conduct. One of them, Eleazar, doubtless expressing the general views of those present, said, 'Since thou desirest to know the truth, if thou wilt be righteous in earnest, lay down the high-priesthood, and content thyself with the civil government of the people.' When pressed for a reason, he aroused the anger of Hyrcanus by a slander on his mother. Hyrcanus was alienated from the Pharisees because they were not willing to punish the offender according to his deserts. The successor of Hyrcanus, Aristobulus, is shown to have been pro-Sadducean if only by the title of 'Philhellene' which he bore. The larger outlook and foreign contacts of the aristocracy obviously brought them into a different atmosphere from that of the Pharisees and the bulk of the people. The unpopularity of Alexander Jannaeus is clearly seen in an incident at the Feast of Tabernacles. Officiating as high-priest, an office which remained throughout, as we have seen,

---

[1] G. H. Box, following the Talmud instead of Josephus, refers it to the reign of Jannaeus. (*Ency. of Religion and Ethics*, Vol. IX, p. 831.)

the basis of the Hasmonaean authority, Alexander poured the libation of water on the ground instead of on the altar, a breach of the Pharisaic tradition. Those present were so indignant that they pelted their high-priest with the citrons which they carried as part of the ritual. A large number of them were forthwith massacred by his soldiers. This ill-feeling took more dangerous form when Alexander suffered a reverse whilst fighting the Arabs across the Jordan. Civil war broke out, in which Alexander used Greek mercenaries against the Jews, and the Jews went so far as to bring in the Seleucid king to help them, and Alexander was defeated. But a revulsion of feeling against the threatened Syrian predominance led to the support of Alexander by many Jews, so that he was able to overcome those who remained irreconcilable. He is said to have celebrated his victory by crucifying 800 of his enemies before the eyes of himself and his harem, whilst the rest fled. Of course, this conflict went far beyond the usual limits of Pharisaic opposition to the Hasmonaeans; and from this point onwards the Pharisees themselves did not resort to arms. But their hatred for Jannaeus is shown by the festival that was observed on the anniversary of his death.

On his death-bed, Jannaeus is said to have advised his wife, Alexandra, to come to terms with the Pharisees as the only possible condition of ruling the country in peace. She acted on this advice, and her reign was a golden age in the Pharisaic tradition. The outstanding Pharisee was her own brother, Simon ben Shetach. Under Queen Alexandra her son Hyrcanus was high-priest, and the Pharisees controlled him; all was done according to their traditions. They were not content with this, however, but sought reprisals on their Sadducean opponents, who found their spokesman and defender in the younger son of Alexandra, Aristobulus. As a compromise, most of the fortresses were given into Sadducean hands, which, of course, prepared for the supremacy of the Sadducees under the rule of Aristobulus, after Alexandra's death.

She should have been succeeded by Hyrcanus, as elder son, but he was attacked by Aristobulus, and forced to yield up both the kingship and the high-priesthood. This is the point at which emerges the highly important figure of Antipater the Idumaean. His father, Antipas, had been made governor of Idumaea by Alexander Jannaeus, and he himself succeeded to this post. He convinced the weak Hyrcanus that his brother, Aristobulus, had designs upon his life, and persuaded him to take refuge with the Nabataean Arabs in Petra. Aretas their king was induced to invade Judaea on behalf of Hyrcanus, as a result of which invasion, Aristobulus was defeated and fled to Jerusalem, where he was besieged by Aretas and Hyrcanus, with the support of many Jews. This was the situation when the Romans intervened.

The Roman Intervention. The real reason for this was an important change in Roman policy. The old Republic was breaking up, and the nationalistic policy of the Senatorial party was being replaced by the imperialistic policy of the military adventurers who form the transition to the rise of the Roman Empire. This meant that the old methods of diplomatic influence without military intervention were changed for those of acquisition and control. Pompey aimed at extending the Roman rule to the Euphrates, and this aim did not allow of civil war in Judaea. Pompey's general, Scaurus, accordingly ordered Aretas and Hyrcanus to abandon the siege, and Aristobulus was left in possession for a couple of years longer. In 63, when Pompey arrived at Damascus, there was an appeal of all parties to him. Not only did both Aristobulus and Hyrcanus plead against each other, but the people, that is the Pharisaic party which led them, pleaded significantly against both. 'We do not wish,' they said, 'to be under kingly government, because the form of government we received from our forefathers was that of subjection to the priests of that God whom they worshipped.'[1] No immediate decision was given, but Aristobulus lost his case by precipitate action. Pompey marched on Jerusalem

[1] Josephus, *Antiquities*, XIV, iii, 2.

and Aristobulus personally surrendered to him, but his Sadducean followers stood a siege of three months in the temple, the city itself being surrendered by the partisans of Hyrcanus. In 63, the temple mount was captured, and Pompey made his famous visit to the Holy of Holies.

IX.—THE JEWS UNDER THE ROMANS

1. FROM POMPEY TO HEROD

BETWEEN Pompey's intervention in 63 and the effective accession of Herod the Great to the throne in 37, there lies a quarter of a century of crowded history, not at all easy to follow, if only because the fate of the Jews was so entangled with the kaleidoscopic changes in Roman affairs. We must be content to single out the salient features alone, and the first thing is to grasp the purpose and problems of the Roman administration in Palestine.

(1) The importance of the Roman province of Syria, of which the Jewish territory in the south formed but a small portion, was that it constituted a convenient, indeed necessary, line of defence on the eastern frontier against such powers as the Parthians. The fertile territory of Syria was not more than seventy to a hundred miles broad, but it extended all along the eastern coast of the Mediterranean, i.e., for about four hundred miles, divided roughly into halves by the mountain ranges of Lebanon and Anti-Lebanon. Internally, the most significant fact was its lack of unity in population and interest. There was a sharp distinction between the rural and urban populations. The Jews, apart from those in Jerusalem, were largely rural in life and occupation; nearly all the cities were Greek. Further, as we have seen throughout the whole course of the history of Israel, Syria was constantly open to invasion, and was therefore likely to be affected by all the military movements and dynastic changes of its neighbours.

The problem which faced Pompey was in some respects comparable with that which faced our own administration of

Palestine, with its racial and religious division and sharp animosities of Jews and Arabs. He tried to solve it by withdrawing from Jewish control most of the Hellenistic cities along the coast, and in Samaria and in the north-east;[1] Judaea was thus left with Idumaea, Galilee, and some of the territory east of Jordan. Over this, he installed Hyrcanus II, not as king, but as high-priest and ethnarch.

(2) Such political conditions were relatively satisfactory to the Pharisees, who from now onwards exercise the dominant religious influence. Their quietism is reflected in the important document known as 'The Psalms of Solomon', which really continue and resemble many of our canonical psalms. They emphasize the contrast between 'sinners', evidently the Sadducees, and the true worshippers of Yahweh, viz., the Pharisees. They look for the coming of the promised Messianic king, who would be installed and supported by divine power, and not by the worldly methods of the reprobated Hasmonaeans. The unnamed conqueror in the Psalms of Solomon is Pompey, who comes from the west and carries off his captives thither (as Pompey did Aristobulus and his sons) and is met with a resistance which he overcomes by bringing up battering-rams against Zion. Finally he is killed in Egypt (which carries down Psalm 2 at least to 48 B.C.).

(3) But this quietistic attitude was by no means shared by all the people, as is shown by the series of unsuccessful revolts made by Aristobulus and his sons, which must have attracted many supporters in the hope of a renewal of national independence. One of the sons, viz., Alexander, who had escaped from captivity, led a revolt in 57; in the following year, Aristobulus and his other son, Antigonus, who had also escaped, led another; in the next year Alexander tried again, and in 52 there was yet another revolt under a certain Pitholaus. None of these were successful, but they are all significant. It was in consequence of the first that

[1] See the map in Oesterley, *History of Israel*, p. 330.

Gabinius, the proconsul in charge, altered the administration, by depriving Hyrcanus of his secular authority, and by dividing the Judaean territory into five districts, under separate control.

(4) The interaction with Roman history, to which reference has been made, is seen in the fact that many of the great Roman leaders of that age figure for a longer or shorter period in Jewish history also. In 54 Crassus, on his way to the fatal campaign against the Parthians, stopped to plunder the Temple. Caesar, after overcoming Pompey (at Pharsalus in 48), was in difficulties at Alexandria, out of which he was helped by Antipater and Jewish forces. This led Caesar to show great favour to Antipater in particular and to the Jews in general, so that they more than any other group mourned his assassination. Cassius withdrew to Syria, of which he was proconsul, and taxed it heavily. When Cassius and Brutus were overthrown at Philippi, the East (including Syria) passed into the hands of Antony, who made Herod and Phasael (the sons of Antipater) tetrarchs under the ethnarch, Hyrcanus II. Through all these changes, Antipater was the power controlling the relation of the Jews to the Romans; his great ability was matched by his great unpopularity with the Jews, as being an Idumaean, and no true Jew. His enemies poisoned him after the overthrow of Cassius.

(5) It was not until 41 that Antigonus found the opportunity to make a new attempt at revolt. It was given through an invasion of Syria by the Parthians, nominally in the republican interest, and against Antony. Antigonus bribed the Parthians to support him, and was by them installed as king in Jerusalem. Hyrcanus was taken captive into Parthia, Phasael (the brother of Herod) was driven to commit suicide in prison, and Herod narrowly escaped capture. He went to Rome, and to his own surprise was appointed king by the Senate, apparently because his strong personality and the record of his father suggested that he was well-fitted to deal with the turbulent Judaea. A Roman army drove out the Parthians, but Herod was not able to overcome

Antigonus, who could claim to be in the genuine Hasmonaean line, as against Herod the Idumaean—though Herod had strengthened his position by his betrothal to Mariamme, the grand-daughter of Hyrcanus. Finally, in 37, a Roman army enabled Herod to capture Jerusalem after a siege of three months, and Antigonus, the last of the Hasmonaean kings, was executed. So began the effective kingship of Herod the Great.

2. HEROD THE GREAT

It is a striking testimony to the power of a single personality, when sufficiently dominating, that Herod should have maintained his position as King of the Jews for a whole generation in times of world-disorder and dramatic changes of world-rule, whilst himself hated by most of the Jews as an Idumaean usurper. We have already seen that he owed his position to the Roman Senate, at the instance of Antony and Octavian (40 B.C.), but it was not until 37 B.C. that the capture of Jerusalem from Antigonus by Roman aid enabled him actually to begin his reign. His first emergence into the light of history had been his appointment by his father Antipater to the governorship of Galilee at the age of twenty-five (c. 49 B.C.). His vigorous action against brigands, and his undaunted bearing before the jealous and hostile Sanhedrin[1] when they called him to account, indicate part of his personal equipment for his long and difficult task. But to the courage and strength and skill of a soldier he added the arts of the diplomatist and the flatteries of a courtier, whenever it was worth his while to employ them towards those in a superior position; to his inferiors he could be ruthless beyond measure. His ruling instinct was the passion for power, power at any cost; his policy in the attainment of it was consistent throughout, for he saw that he could gain and keep power only by the consent and support of the Romans. He was not less adroit than his father, Antipater, in transferring his

[1] *Schürer* II, 1907, pp. 237ff.; *Eng. Trans.* Div. II, Vol. I, pp. 163ff.

allegiance from one dominating ruler to another; Herod made himself as indispensable to Octavian (Augustus) after Actium in 31, as he had been to Antony before it, and he was on terms of personal intimacy with Marcus Agrippa, the presumptive successor of Augustus.

By general consent, the reign of Herod falls into three distinct parts, the first being that of the consolidation of his power from 37 to 25, the second that of the prosperous exercise of it, especially through lavish expenditure on buildings and benefactions at home and abroad, which lasted from 25 to 13, the third that of the domestic tragedies for which his own passionate and suspicious nature was primarily responsible, 13–4 B.C.

(1) *The Consolidation of his Power.* The overthrow of Antigonus, and his execution by the Romans at the desire of Herod, still left Herod face to face with the former supporters of Antigonus. Forty-five of these he killed (XV, i, 2),[1] and he used the wealth of his enemies to ensure the favour of Antony and his other friends. This was a heavy blow to the Sadducean party, one, in fact, from which it never recovered fully; the Sanhedrin loses all importance during the whole reign of Herod. It was an exact fulfilment of the warning given to the Sanhedrin by Sameas (Shemaiah) when Herod as governor of Galilee had been summoned before them, and they were afraid to act against him (XIV, ix, 4). This Shemaiah, with his teacher, Pollio (Abtalion), had urged the surrender of Jerusalem to Herod before its capture, in accordance with the Pharisaic 'quietism' which they represented. This does not mean that the Pharisees approved of Herod, but that they regarded him as an instrument of divine wrath against the sins of the age. Their quietistic attitude enabled Herod to keep on relatively good terms with them, and he even abstained from any punishment of the Pharisees who refused to take the oath of allegiance to him (XV, x, 4). Such leniency was, of course, politic, because of their influence with the ordinary people. Herod had plenty of enemies in

[1] This and the following references are to the *Antiquities* of Josephus.

L

those who sought a restoration of the Hasmonaeans, without making the Pharisees into active foes.

Herod's position was that of a *rex socius*, 'by gift of Caesar and by decree of the Senate' (XV, vi, 7); it gave him full authority (except for coinage) within his dominions, but none to wage war or make treaties with other states, whilst he was bound to supply troops or monetary support on demand. On the other hand, as we have repeatedly seen, the internal authority of the Hasmonaeans depended on their tenure of the high-priestly office, to which Herod, as an Idumaean, could not aspire. His father, Antipater, had made use of Hyrcanus II as figure-head, but Hyrcanus had been carried off by the Parthians. Herod secured his return to Judaea, though the mutilation he had suffered at the hands of Antigonus prevented him from resuming the office of high-priest. Accordingly Herod replaced him by an obscure priest from Babylon, named Ananel (XV, ii, 4). This action roused Alexandra, the daughter of the aged Hyrcanus, and widow of Alexander, the son of Aristobulus II; she urged Antony through Cleopatra to secure the office for her own son, Aristobulus III. His sister, Mariamme, the wife of Herod, aided Alexandra in putting pressure on Herod, who eventually yielded, but had the young high-priest murdered within the first year of his appointment (XV, iii, 3).

Cleopatra's hostility to Herod was a serious obstacle to him, owing to her influence with Antony; she made him suffer in his revenues, as well as in other ways. Antony transferred to her a good deal of the Phoenician and Philistine coast, with some Arabian territory, and in particular, the fertile district about Jericho, for which Herod had to pay tribute to her, though it properly belonged to his own domains. Herod and Cleopatra were well matched—when she had occasion to pass through Judaea, she tried to ensnare him in the net of her charms, whilst he was seriously considering whether he should not rid himself of her by his favourite method of assassination. The dependence of the future history of the world on the relations of this absolutely unprincipled pair is suggestive (XV, iv, 2), and raises interesting questions for a philosophy of history.

Herod's path was cleared by the death of Cleopatra as a sequel to the battle of Actium (31). But this left him in a difficult position as one of Antony's supporters over against the victor, Octavian. Fortunately for Herod, he had been occupied against his will in an Arabian war to collect tribute for Cleopatra, so that he had not been directly engaged against Octavian. He also found an early opportunity of rendering him some help, before going personally to offer his services to the victor. But Herod's unprincipled cunning is seen in the fact that before leaving Judaea he had Hyrcanus —now more than eighty years of age—executed on a false charge by his subservient Sanhedrin. The only reason for this murder of a harmless old man was that it removed a possible figure-head substitute for himself, if he could not insinuate himself into Octavian's good graces. There is no reason to think that Octavian was deceived as to the character of Herod; but it was as much to Octavian's advantage as to Herod's that Palestine should be in the hands of a *rex socius*. It formed a very useful frontier-state for a ruler who had no intention of extending the Roman power beyond the Euphrates, and it was obviously less trouble to leave such a state in the hands of a native or semi-native king, provided he were sufficiently strong, than to administer it directly from Rome. The *sine qua non* was that the king should be able to keep order in his own state, and this Herod was pre-eminently able to do by his ruthless methods. It was only because there was no second Herod that Judaea fell into the hands of Roman procurators so soon after his death. As a result of this Roman policy Octavian actually increased Herod's territory, both now and a few years later (in 23), so that he eventually ruled over the whole of Palestine, except the Decapolis (the Bashan-Gilead district east of Jordan, with Scythopolis-Beth-shean west of it) and the sea-coast to the north of Caesarea (XV, vii, 3 and XV, x, 1).

It was not long after the successful establishment of Herod

in the favour of Octavian that Herod's passionately loved
wife, Mariamme, fell a victim to his suspicions and the
intrigues of the palace. Her outspokenness about the treatment of her relatives had temporarily alienated him, and
Salome, the sister of Herod, seized the opportunity to con-
coct the charge that she was attempting to poison him. In
his rage he had Mariamme executed, only to regret her loss
wildly and bitterly. This was in 29; in the following year,
Herod's serious illness and expected death led Alexandra (the
mother of Mariamme) to take steps towards securing control
of Jerusalem. When this was reported to Herod, he had her
executed. In 25 Herod exterminated the last of the Hasmonaeans (the sons of Babas) who could be put forward as
his rivals. This event marks the close of the first period of
Herod's reign, that of the consolidation of his power. From
this point onwards that power, however deeply resented, was
never really challenged (XV, vii, 10).

(2) *Prosperity—Buildings, Benefactions and Hellenistic
Culture.* The lavish expenditure and costly munificence of
Herod during the middle period of his reign is entirely consistent with that passion for power at any cost of bloodshed
which we have seen in the first period. He was a man who in
any case liked to do things magnificently that he might shine
by the brilliance of his benefactions; he was always capable
of a gesture that in any other man might be called generosity.
Thus in 25, during a severe famine, he melted down all the
gold and silver plate of his palace to buy corn from Egypt for
his people (XV, ix, 2); in 20, during another time of dearth,
he remitted a third of the taxation (XV, x, 4); in 14, after the
visit of M. Agrippa to Judaea, and his own assiduous attend-
ance upon Agrippa (the presumptive successor of Augustus)
in Asia Minor, he celebrated his return by remitting a fourth
part of the taxation (XVI, ii, 5). But Herod's expenditure
was usually directed to such particular objects as furthered
his own policy. In this way we can explain the erection of
fortresses against brigands at home and against plundering
Bedouin on the frontiers, the elaborate and very costly

artificial harbour at Caesarea, which eventually made it, after Herod's time, the most important city in Palestine, and the rebuilding of Samaria (Sebaste). Amongst his buildings, that of the Temple naturally takes the foremost place. By means of elaborate substructures, still to be seen, he doubled the Temple area, north and south, and re-built the existent Temple on a scale worthy of such a king, and in a manner capable of arousing the admiration of even the disciples of Jesus. In all this work, which took from eight to ten years, and indeed went on almost till the time of the destruction of the Temple in the next century, Herod was at the greatest pains to avoid any offence to the religious convictions of his subjects; none knew better than he what trouble these could bring to a ruler (XV, ii, 1f.). This consideration, dictated purely by questions of policy, was confined to Judaea. Herod the Idumaean was, says Josephus, 'more friendly to the Greeks than to the Jews' (XIX, vii, 3), and the Greeks formed a very considerable part of his kingdom. He cultivated friendly relations with them in the Greek cities of his land and abroad, as he did with the more open-minded Jews of the Diaspora. Like other kings and rulers, he fell into line with the Roman policy of unification through Graeco-Roman culture, the direct descendant of the old Hellenistic movement. He had at his court Nicolas of Damascus, the historian, and other Greek scholars; he established theatres and buildings for the Greek games and he endowed heathen temples. He seems to have been as popular as an autocratic ruler of those times could well be, outside the strictly Jewish population of Judaea, where even the gift of a new Temple could not reconcile the Jew to his Idumaean birth. He used his influence on behalf of Jews in Greek cities, and even in Galilee his relation to the very mixed population was different from that to the Judaeans. There is no reason to doubt that for most of his subjects his reign was a time of prosperity; the horrible tale of palace-plots and murders which fills so large a place in the pages of Josephus, must not hide this from us.

(3) *Domestic Troubles* (13–4 B.C.). The closing period of Herod's reign fitly rounds off his career of crime, and indeed powerfully illustrates the great moral inevitabilities, which are as stern and relentless in their dealing with men as are those of nature. At an earlier stage, his own passion and suspicion had made him an easy prey to those who robbed him of Mariamme; once more, he was to be misled by traitors of his own family, into the murder of Mariamme's sons, Alexander and Aristobulus. In 23, he had sent them to Rome for their education in the house of Asinius Pollio (XV, x, 1); he brought them back in 18–17 B.C. (XVI, i, 2), and clearly intended them to be his successors. This roused the jealousy and fear of Salome, the sister of Herod, who tried at first to turn their father against them by false reports. She and her party so far succeeded that Herod brought back to his court a son by his first wife, Doris, viz., Antipater, and eventually sent Antipater to Rome with Agrippa, for introduction to Augustus. The plots and false charges of Antipater eventually led Herod to complain to Caesar about Alexander and Aristobulus, but Augustus temporarily reconciled the father and his sons. There could be no peace or good understanding, however, in such an atmosphere as that of Herod's palace. Once more the father's mind was poisoned against his son Alexander, and Herod imprisoned him, but again there was a reconciliation. A third time, however, Herod was induced to believe that Alexander and Aristobulus were plotting against his life, and now obtained permission from Augustus to proceed fully against them, with the result that they were strangled at Sebaste (7 B.C.). Well might Augustus say that it was better to be Herod's pig than his son. Antipater, who had for a time replaced them, suffered the punishment which he amply deserved. His father had made him his successor, but finally discovered his undoubted treachery, and the part he had played in securing the death of his half-brothers; Antipater was recalled from Rome to trial and execution, just five days before Herod himself died of a loathsome and agonizing

disease. Salome, the other arch-plotter of the palace, survived Herod. It was characteristic of the half-mad king to summon the principal men of his kingdom to his death-bed, and to have them imprisoned, whilst Salome was ordered to have them put to death at the same time as he himself died, that there might be an ample mourning of the nation to mark his own departure. Salome did not act on this command.

How all these things were regarded by religious men may be seen best from the pseudepigraphical book known as 'The Assumption of Moses'. This was written soon after the death of Herod and the succession of his sons, and sets forth the attitude of a Pharisaic quietist, waiting for the Messianic judgment. After speaking of the Maccabees and Hasmonaeans, who called themselves priests and worked iniquity in the holy of holies, it goes on:

'And an insolent king shall succeed them, who will not be of the race of the priests, a man bold and shameless, and he shall judge them as they shall deserve. And he shall cut off their chief men with the sword, and shall destroy them in secret places, so that no one may know where their bodies are. He shall slay the old and the young, and he shall not spare. Then the fear of him shall be bitter in their land. And he shall execute judgments on them as the Egyptians executed upon them, during thirty and four years, and he shall punish them.'[1]

Thus religious faith can interpret the worst of men as the scourge of God, and find a place for them in the divine Providence.

3. The Herodian Kings

From the death of Herod the Great to the destruction of Jerusalem covers three-quarters of a century. This period is of peculiar interest because it forms the immediate background of most of the New Testament. It is divided, rather

---

[1] Translation by Charles in *Apocrypha and Pseudepigrapha of the Old Testament*, Vol. II, p. 418.

more than half-way, by the brief rule of Herod Agrippa I, under whom the country was united (41–44), as it had been in the days of Herod the Great, his grandfather. Before him we have a division of the country under the three sons of Herod, followed (in the case of Judaea) by a succession of procurators for a whole generation. After Agrippa, Judaea was again governed by procurators for a quarter of a century, until the Jewish War led to the truly epoch-making event of A.D. 70. The interest afforded by our data is partly in the characters of the men who shaped the history, and partly in the illustrations of moral and political cause and effect.

Even before the death of Herod an event occurred which was prophetic of the coming years. The false report of his death led certain Rabbis to incite their more athletic pupils to pull down the golden eagle which Herod had set over the great gate of the Temple. The old king, dying, was still to be reckoned with, and one of his last acts was to order the culprits to be burnt alive. But it was after his death that the serious disturbances began. At Passover there was a tumult in Jerusalem during which many were killed by the soldiers of Archelaus. Another serious disturbance occurred at Pentecost, during which the cloisters of the Temple were burnt and its treasury plundered. There were also revolts in other parts of the country, notably in Galilee, where the Zealots now emerge for the first time, under the leadership of Judas (probably not the Judas of Galilee named in Acts 5:37). The Zealots have been described by Wellhausen as 'the country party'. Their characteristic feature was their use of armed force to overthrow foreign dominion, in contrast with the political quietism of the Pharisees. It is of interest that one of the disciples of Jesus was an ex-Zealot (Simon).

The three sons of Herod, Archelaus, Antipas and Philip, appeared before Augustus for his decision as to the future of the administration; they had to face a Jewish embassy protesting against the rule of any of the Herods, and asking to be governed directly from Rome. Augustus gave his judgment in terms of Herod's third will, though he withheld the title of king from any of the three. According to this arrangement, Archelaus became Ethnarch of Judaea, Samaria and Idumaea; Antipas, Tetrarch of Galilee and Peraea (north-east of the Dead Sea), Philip, Tetrarch of the north-east territory (Batanaea, Trachonitis, Auranitis). Of the three, Antipas ruled longest, and most nearly continued the character and tradition of his father, and we may begin with him, of whom also we have most information. His territory consisted of two distinct and separated parts, north-west and south-east, and the position of Peraea made it open to Arab invasion. For this reason Antipas found it expedient to marry the daughter of Aretas, the king of the Nabataean Arabs. When he became entangled with Herodias (his evil genius) and proposed to divorce the daughter of Aretas, he naturally had trouble with his father-in-law, as well as with the popular Jewish prophet, John the Baptist. The daughter of Aretas returned to her father, who made war on Herod and destroyed his army. Josephus tells us that the Jews regarded this as a just penalty for his treatment of John the Baptist, which treatment Josephus does not, like the Gospels, connect with Herodias (XVIII, v, 2). It was under the jurisdiction of this Herod that most of the teaching of Jesus was given; when friendly Pharisees warned Him of the danger in which He stood from Herod, Jesus signalized his craft by calling him, 'that fox' (Luke 13:32). Antipas, defeated by Aretas, appealed to Rome; he was a favourite of Tiberius, after whom he had named Tiberias, his new capital, but the death of the emperor prevented help from being given. The trouble with Aretas was not the only mischief wrought by Herodias. When Agrippa was installed as king over Philip's former territory in 37, she urged Antipas to appeal to Caligula for the same title as her brother. Agrippa countered this by accusing Herod Antipas of disloyalty, as a result of which he was banished to Gaul, whither Herodias, it should be said, voluntarily accompanied him.

Philip ruled for twenty-seven years over a mixed people, more Syrian and Arab than Jewish. Little is known of him, but that little is good, and he was one of the best of the Herods. But Archelaus, ruling over Judaea (with Idumaea) and Samaria, was certainly the worst of the sons of Herod. After ten years, he was banished as the result of a joint appeal of Jews and Samaritans against him—a highly significant combination.

The story of Herod Agrippa I, under whom the whole land was for a short time again united, reads like a biographical novel. Anyone with sufficient knowledge and imagination to reconstruct it will have before him a vivid picture of the times, the very antithesis of that other world of religious life and thought to which the contemporary New Testament testifies. This Herod was the son of Aristobulus (executed in 7 B.C. by the ever-suspicious Herod), and was thus the grandson of Herod the Great and the Hasmonaean Mariamme. He was sent to Rome in his earlier years for his education, and there became intimate with Drusus, the Emperor's son. His admission into the high society of Rome proved his undoing; he incurred heavy debts, and on the death of his friend was compelled to leave Rome. He seems to have contemplated suicide, but his brother-in-law, Herod Antipas, gave him a very subordinate post at Tiberias, which he kept only for a short time. Many ups and downs followed, and he eventually made his way back to Rome, where he regained his old position on borrowed money, and became intimate with the future emperor, Caligula. Riding in a chariot with him, Agrippa expressed the wish that the emperor Tiberius might soon be out of the way to make room for Caligula. The driver of the chariot, Agrippa's servant, heard what was said, and kept quiet, until his master discovered him in theft, whereupon the servant informed against his earlier treasonable words. Tiberius threw Agrippa into prison, where he remained for six months, until the accession of Caligula brought release. Caligula is said to have presented his friend with a chain of gold the exact equivalent in weight to the iron chain which he had worn as a prisoner. This chain Agrippa subsequently dedicated as an offering in the Jewish Temple.

But Caligula's favour was shown in more serviceable ways. In 37, Agrippa was appointed to succeed Philip, who had died some years previously. In 40, the territory of Antipas was added to Philip's, and in 41 Claudius further added the territory of Judaea and Samaria, thus bringing a united rule to all the dominions formerly divided amongst Herod's three sons.

The policy of Agrippa resembled that of our own Charles II; whatever happened he was determined not to go on his travels again. He showed a good deal of his grandfather's shrewdness in dealing with the Jews, and his milder disposition enabled him to get on exceedingly well with them. The dedication of his chain of gold is a symbol of his shrewdness, as is also his good-tempered attitude towards a Pharisee who had demanded his exclusion from the Temple. He summoned the man, talked quietly with him, and dismissed him with a present. The New Testament tells us that his persecution of Christians was dictated by the desire to please the Jews, which is fully in accord with all else we know of him. It is not surprising that the Pharisees found in him a ruler after their own heart. But outside the borders of Judaism he showed himself more of a Hellenist than a Jew; at Berytus, for example, he became equally popular with his Syrian subjects by providing them with musicians and with condemned malefactors for the gladiatorial contests. This was the man who won the flattering plaudits of his subjects at Caesarea, when the sun shone on his silver armour—'a god, not a man' they cried. Both Josephus and the New Testament saw a divine judgment on his acceptance of this adoration in the illness which removed him within five days.[1]

[1] Acts 12:23; *Ant*, XIX, viii, 2. He is not to be confused with his son, the second Agrippa, who eventually succeeded to part of his northern territory, but had little influence on subsequent events. It is this second Agrippa before whom Paul appeared, and who jestingly replied to Paul's earnest appeal, 'With a little persuasion thou wouldst fain make me a Christian.'

4. THE ROMAN PROCURATORS

On the removal of Archelaus from Judaea and Samaria in A.D. 6, these territories had fallen into the hands of Roman procurators, men of the equestrian or middle-class order, and not, therefore, of the same class as the Syrian legates, who were of senatorial rank. The procurators, however, seem to have possessed relative independence until any point was reached at which the Syrian legate might have to act. We notice again and again the ignorance of Jewish religion shown by the procurators, and their frequent injustice and corrupt dealing. Their administrative centre was Caesarea, where the troops were chiefly stationed—non-Jewish, though recruited locally. The Procurator was a military officer, retaining in his hands the power of life and death. He was responsible for the imperial finance, as distinct from the customs duties. The imperial finance, unlike the customs, was not farmed out, and was collected from the eleven toparchies; it included both a land tax and a head tax. All other matters were dealt with by the self-government of the Jews through the aristocratic Sanhedrin and the district councils. This payment of tribute direct to 'Caesar' was a new and irritating practice, part of the price paid by the Jews for being delivered from Herodian rule in Judaea, according to their often expressed wish.

Even apart from the Gospel incidents, the best-known of the procurators of this first period (of whom there were seven) is Pontius Pilate. In the Gospels he is shown as a weak and hesitating official, but this is not the impression we gain from other sources. His general conduct was aggressive, and showed little fear of, or regard for, the Jewish people. On one occasion he arbitrarily provoked the people by bringing the Roman standards (bearing the image of the Emperor) into Jerusalem. Even when his actions were really beneficial, as in the provision of a better water-supply for Jerusalem, he managed to provoke riots over it. His dismissal came through his high-handed conduct in regard to the Samaritans, who successfully appealed against him.

The only other incidents of the period calling for notice arose through the proposal of Caligula to establish the Caesarian cult in Jerusalem. He ordered Petronius, the legate of Syria, to set up a statue of himself in the Temple. Petronius, who knew the Jews far better than his master, was in a difficult position. To carry out the proposal would have meant a terrible rebellion, anticipating the events of later years; to refuse to execute it certainly meant death for himself. Fortunately the interposition of Herod Agrippa, who had the ear of Caligula, persuaded him to cancel his order. As we have already seen, the government of Judaea passed in A.D. 41 for several years into Herod Agrippa's hands from those of the procurators. During the twenty-two years before the outbreak of the Jewish War it was in the hands of another series of seven procurators (44–66). It is easy for us, in retrospect, to see the cumulative force of events arising on the one hand from the stubborn determination of the Jews to resist any encroachment on what they considered their religious privileges, and on the other, from the misgovernment of these Roman officials, due either to the want of sympathetic understanding or to their positive corruption and injustice. It is strange that in this long succession there were not men of higher character and ability, though this fact illustrates the need for a new religion in the contemporary world. The first, *Cuspus Fadus*, foolishly deprived the Jews of the charge of the high-priestly garments, which had been yielded to them by a wiser Roman. The second, *Tiberius Alexander*, could hardly have been an acceptable governor, since he was an apostate from his native Judaism. The third, *Ventidius Cumanus*, inflicted heavy slaughter in quelling a Passover riot, which had been started by the indecent act of a Roman soldier in the Temple courts. At another time, he punished an assault on a Roman official by plundering the neighbouring villages. In the course of this plundering a roll of the Law was torn up with contempt

and insult by a soldier; the disturbance this created had to be
settled by the execution of the offender. Finally Cumanus
took such action in regard to strife between the Jews and the
Samaritans as to provoke an appeal to the Syrian legate, and
to lead ultimately to the banishment of the procurator himself. The fourth procurator, *Felix*, is known to us from the
New Testament as Paul's judge at Caesarea, and also from
the biting sentence of Tacitus, with reference to his being a
freedman: 'per omnem saevitiam ac libidinem jus regium
servili ingenio exercuit'—'in every way of cruelty and lust he
used a king's power in a slave's spirit.' It has been said of
him that he marks the critical point in the whole sequence;
the conduct of Felix made a pacific settlement henceforth
impossible. In his time of office we see not only the growth of
the Zealots, but the rise of the Sicarii, assassins in a patriotic
interest, who literally as well as figuratively formed the
dagger-point of the Zealots. His successor, *Porcius Festus*,
was a man of better type, but came too late. The chief
impression left by the next procurator, *Albinus*, was his
greed for money. So we reach the last of the procurators,
Gessius Florus, and apparently the worst, under whom the
long checked outbreak occurred.

5. The Jewish War

The great rebellion of the Jews, which ultimately brought
against them the full force of the Roman Empire, extended
over four years, and was marked by scenes of the wildest
ferocity that the world has ever seen, including fierce civil
war amongst the Jews themselves. To find any parallel we
should have to turn to the worst parts of the French Revolution or of the Russian overthrow of Czarism. No doubt the
statistics of Josephus are often exaggerated, but his full and
precise details as to many of the massacres and deeds of
ruthless cruelty cannot have been invented. His account of
the conflict in the early stages, in which he himself took a
prominent part, is given at great length in his *Jewish War*.

The events of the war fall into four divisions, viz.:

(1) From the aggressive acts of Florus (64–66) to the defeat of the Syrian legate, Gallus, in 66.

(2) The subjugation of Galilee by Vespasian in 67.

(3) The Civil War in Jerusalem and Vespasian's campaign, 68–69.

(4) The capture of Jerusalem by Titus in 70.

The actual occasion of the outbreak was at Caesarea, where the Jews were dominated by the Greeks; it was a dispute about the right of way to a synagogue. The folly of Florus fanned the spark to a flame; he was irritated because his rapacity had been mocked by someone taking up a collection 'for the poor procurator', and his irritation issued in the killing, scourging and crucifying of a number of Jews. The endeavours of the Syrian legate and of Agrippa II to stay the rebellion were useless, and the definite declaration of war began with the refusal to continue the usual sacrifices for the Emperor in the temple. The pacifists were overcome, and the rebellion extended over the whole country. The Syrian legate marched against Jerusalem; to the surprise of everyone, he then withdrew and was attacked and defeated by the Jews. This temporary victory was a real misfortune to the Jews, since it swept many who stood aloof over to the side of the belligerents.

Josephus was appointed to a command in Galilee, where John of Gischala was leading the Zealots. One of the most important places there, Sepphoris, surrendered to the Romans without fighting. After the fall of Jotapata, commanded by Josephus, he saved his life by assuming the rôle of a prophet, and by flattering Vespasian. John escaped from Gischala and made his way to Jerusalem.

Jerusalem itself became the scene of civil war. John of Gischala established himself in the Temple court and called in the Idumaeans to help him against the more moderate party, who thereupon called in another Zealot, Simon bar Giora, to help them against John. There were now three factions of the more violent type, viz., Eleazar, holding the inner temple, John of Gischala, the temple hill and the castle of Antonia, and Simon bar Giora, the upper city. Vespasian deliberately left them to waste their strength on each other, whilst he continued to reduce the rest of the country. When the call to be emperor came from his troops, he left the operations in Judaea to his son, Titus, who eventually captured Jerusalem, after a siege lasting from April to September of A.D. 70. When the outer walls, the castle of Antonia and the Temple had fallen, John and Simon were still fighting each other in the Upper City, Eleazar having been eliminated at an earlier stage. In 71, Titus celebrated his triumph in Rome, of which the famous Arch of Titus remains a memorial, but until 73 there were still isolated fortresses to be reduced. Jerusalem was razed to the ground, and though there were further outbreaks of Jews in Egypt and Cyrene, Cyprus and Mesopotamia under Trajan (115–117), and a rebellion of Palestinian Jews under Hadrian (132–135)—the Bar-Kochba revolt—it was the destruction of Jerusalem in 70 which marked the real end of the history of Israel as a people centred in a common land and sharing a common political life.

6. The Dispersion

Many Jewish prisoners were taken away by the Romans after the capture of Jerusalem in A.D. 70, but there was no policy of deportation. The dispersion of Jews throughout the Mediterranean world had been going on for centuries, as we have already seen, and by the time of the Christian era, it had become very extensive in area and in numbers. In John 7:35, we have a significant reference to this 'Diaspora'; the Jews are represented as saying of Jesus, 'Whither will this man go, that we shall not find Him? Will he go unto the Dispersion among the Greeks and teach the Greeks?' (Cf. James 1:1; 1 Peter 1:1.) This reference is significant not only for the fact, but also for the character of the Dispersion. Its centre of gravity, at least for the Western world, was Alexandria, and its language was Greek, the universal language of the early Empire. It is true that there was also a large Eastern dispersion centred in Mesopotamia and dating from the Exile, but of the history of this we know comparatively little until we reach the centuries in which the Talmud came into being. For our present purpose we are concerned with this more western dispersion, speaking Greek.

At the time of the Christian era, according to Philo, there was a large number of Jews in Egypt and Syria, in Asia Minor, in Greece, in the Mediterranean islands and in the Euphrates district. Even before this date, according to the Sibylline Oracles, c. 140 B.C., the Jews are said to be everywhere. In Syria the headquarters were naturally Antioch and Damascus; in fact we have a reference to a trading colony of Jews in Damascus as early as the ninth century B.C. (1 Kings 20:34). As for Asia Minor we know that Antiochus the Great (c. 198) deported two thousand Jewish families thither from Babylonia and Mesopotamia, and according to 1 Macc. 15:15–24 (Roman letters to many peoples) there was already a wide diffusion of Jews there by the first century B.C. We have the fullest data in regard to Egypt; after the fall of Jerusalem in 586 B.C. a body of Jews migrated to Egypt, taking with them Jeremiah. The Epistle of Aristeas (13) implies that Jewish soldiers served in Egypt in the sixth century, and the Elephantine Papyri (see page 122) show that such Jews with a military organization were already settled in Elephantine when Cambyses came into Egypt. The most important event in the history of Egyptian Judaism was the founding of Alexandria by Alexander, who incorporated the Jews as citizens in this new settlement. A little later, after Ptolemy Lagi had captured Jerusalem, he deported a number of prisoners to Egypt. The Jews possessed a special quarter (north-east) in Alexandria, and in Philo's time are said to have numbered a million, roughly two-fifths of the population of Alexandria, and one-eighth of that of Egypt. Another point in the history of Egyptian Judaism is the founding of the temple of Leontopolis about

M

160 by Onias.[1] This temple existed until the Romans closed
it in A.D. 73. Altogether, it will be seen that Egypt in general,
and Alexandria in particular, were the effective headquarters
of the Greek dispersion, though this does not mean that
Jerusalem had been out-rivalled in their affections. As to
the other countries mentioned by Philo, we have much
detailed evidence of the presence of Jews in Cyrenaica and
North Africa, in Macedonia and Greece and in Rome, where
we hear of propaganda at the time of Simon's embassy.
Roman Judaism was also strengthened by the prisoners
deported by Pompey, many of whom would ultimately be
made freedmen. The evidence as to other countries of the
Roman world chiefly belongs to the later Empire. Juster,
our chief authority for the condition of the Jews in the
Roman Empire, estimates that there were in it between six
and seven millions of Jews before A.D. 70. It is not easy to
estimate the precise causes for this remarkable growth,
though it is easy enough to see what they were in general.
The Jews themselves were a prolific race, they were ardent
propagandists as long as they had free course for propaganda,
and theirs seem to have been the first religion to employ
missionaries effectively, at any rate in the western world.[2]
The missionary zeal of Judaism is reflected in Matt. 23:15:
'Ye compass sea and land to make one proselyte.' In addition
to such argumentative propaganda, there had been also the
forcible incorporation of people of other beliefs within
Judaism during the period of the Hasmonaean power,
notably in Edom and Galilee (enforced mass-conversion).

[1] Described by Josephus (*Jewish War*, VII, x, 3). Onias was the
son of the last legitimate high-priest at Jerusalem (Onias III) and took
this step when he saw no prospect of succession there. His action was
naturally not fully approved by the Jews of Palestine; cf. Mishnah,
Menahoth, xiii, 10.

[2] Juster, *Les Juifs dans l'Empire Romain*, Vol. I, p. 254. See also
E. Bevan's essay 'Hellenistic Judaism' in *The Legacy of Israel*.

X.—ISRAEL'S CONTRIBUTION TO THE
PHILOSOPHY OF HISTORY

In the Isle of Oxney there is an incense-altar of the god
Mithra. In far-off days it gathered up the aspirations of
Roman legionaries; in later centuries it served as a mounting-
block for horsemen; to-day it is an object of antiquarian
interest that has found sanctuary in a Christian church.
Some might see in that stone an epitome of the inevitable
course of the history of religion—first, an ardent cult, then a
social factor, and finally a memorial of antiquity. But we
may also see in it a symbol of something more universal and
more permanent—a symbol of that union of material and
spiritual factors which makes all history. The quarried stone
gains a new significance from the men who use it, whether
in the high use of religious faith, or the lower use of social
utility; it becomes at once the concrete expression of human
life and the effective instrument of human consciousness. So
is it with the material and spiritual factors of all human
history.

The ultimate unity of these factors was asserted in the
opening paragraph of this book. The nature and position
of a land will dominate the economic life and international
relations of the people that occupies it; the political and
religious organizations and ideas will express what the people
is, and shape what it shall become. The two sets of factors,
material and spiritual, blend as subtly and as inextricably as
do body and soul. To that blending are due the peculiar
difficulty and fascination of the problems of history, as
distinct from nature-study on the one hand and pure metaphysics on the other. We may gain an apparent unity by

concentrating on one or the other group of factors, and so with Marx reduce all history to changes in the modes of production and exchange, or with Hegel to the realization of the Absolute Idea. But to make the past 'orb into the perfect star' in this one-sided way is to make something which 'men saw not when they moved therein', and something which our personal experience of life should prevent us from ever seeing.

We have seen that in Israel's history both groups of factors are conspicuous and characteristic. On the one hand, the hills of Palestine made it always a land of tribes, or sectional groups, whilst the nature of the soil and the immediate environment of desert brought two distinct kinds of culture, the nomadic and the agricultural, into continued opposition. Moreover, the well-known position of Palestine, on the highway between the world-empires of Egypt and Mesopotamia, made it both a battle-ground of rival ambitions and a clearing-house of the religious ideas of the nearer East. On the other hand, the racial traditions and previous nomadic life of the Israelites caused their social and religious ideas to be shaped by the conception of 'corporate personality'— an important and often neglected principle of Biblical exegesis. The family, the clan, the tribe, and ultimately the nation, were always conceived as the primary unity, within which the idea of individuality arose but slowly and becomes explicit quite late.[1] This had important consequences both for ethics and for religion. The ethical ideals were strongly social—justice and mercy within the group, and the preservation of the group itself against outside peril. The religion was concerned with the God of the tribe or the nation; even the great prophets dealt with the nation primarily, and only secondarily with the individual members of it. God's concern was with the nation, and the prophets in whom the religious consciousness of the nation becomes articulate are at once the representatives of the nation before God, gathering it up

[1] See Lecture VI, 'The Group and the Individual in Israel', in the volume *The Individual in East and West* (ed. by E. R. Hughes).

into their own consciousness, and the live point in the nation at which God made contact with its inner life. In the prophets the material and the spiritual factors were unified.

How far did Israel herself become conscious of the significance of her history? Apparently it was the rise of the monarchy in connection with the overthrow of the Philistine domination of the tribes which first created a national consciousness leading to the writing of history. The beginnings of this literature were made with the events closest at hand, such as we saw in the *Court History of David*; gradually the historian worked backwards, gathering the songs and legends of the past. Then, later on, after the prophets had taught those principles of a theocracy which we have come to call 'Deuteronomic', the historical books were edited in the light of moral retribution, and at last the Pentateuch was co-ordinated to bring out the selective Providence of God in relation to His chosen people, and history, from being as at first descriptive, became didactic.

In the strict sense of the phrase, Israel had no philosophy of history; she never learnt to think in abstract and generalizing ways either of God or of man, or of that history which recorded their relations to each other. Nevertheless, Israel has made a unique contribution to the philosophy of history by the intrinsic qualities of her historic life. Her contribution to the philosophy of *religion* would be admitted by all; it is Israel's monotheism which is the foundation, not only of Christianity and Islam, but also of the very substance of philosophical theism. Hegel himself taught that the picture-method of religion moved in advance of metaphysic. If Greece has given us the conscious logic of thought, Israel has given us much of its subject-matter in these high realms. We may hold with Bergson[1] that 'whilst intelligence treats all things mechanically, instinct proceeds, so to speak, organically. If the consciousness sleeping within instinct awoke, if it were to internalize itself in knowledge, instead of externalizing itself in action, if we knew how to question it,

[1] '*L'Évolution Créatrice*,' p. 179.

M 2

and it could answer, it would betray to us the most intimate
secrets of life.' The object of this chapter is to indicate the
lines along which Israel's instinct moved, in regard to the
nature and meaning, not of religion, but of history, and to
show that her contribution in this respect also is as worthy
of attention as that of the philosophy of religion.

Of the various possible lines of inquiry there are four which
seem to stand out most clearly, not simply because of their
intrinsic importance, but also because they find characteristic
manifestation in the history of Israel. These are (1) the interaction of faith and event, (2) the positive value of the time-
series, (3) the unity of history, (4) the relation of immanence
and transcendence. Incidentally, of course, these features
also serve to bring out certain characteristics of Israel's
religion, though it is not with this, as such, that we are here
primarily concerned.

1. The Interaction of Faith and Event

In the first place, Israel's history shows throughout, and
in several impressive ways, the importance of those psychical
events which have been called the real kernel of history.
When some physical event is regarded as a proof of supernatural intervention or control, there is always a prior belief.
A new fact is constituted by the interpretation of the event
through the belief, and by the confirmation of the belief
through the event. We may see the creation of this new fact,
for example, in the narrative of the Exodus, which had a
place in the religion of Israel comparable with that of the
Cross and the Resurrection in Christianity. The essential
physical events which underlie the narrative were probably
simple enough. A group of nomads on the borders of Egypt
are forced into a labour-levy; after a time they revolt and
make for the desert under a leader; their escape is facilitated
by various calamities in Egypt, and by a wind that drives
back the shallow waters north of Suez, whilst the return of
these waters hinders the Egyptian guards from following
them up. In all this there may have been nothing 'super-

natural' from our point of view, or from that of the Egyptians; the really important fact was the faith that made the escape the permanent symbol of the activity of a redeeming God, who thus became effectively the God of Israel.[1]

The primary faith is expressed by Hosea (12:9):

'I am Yahweh thy God, from the land of Egypt.'

It is to that fact, i.e., to those events interpreted by that faith, that the prophets point Israel for the renewal of her faith amid contemporary needs. It is that fact in which we can most clearly see the difference between Israel's religion and that of all other nations of the nearer East. For these, God and people were linked inseparably by a quasi-physical relation; but Yahweh is a God of History, who freely chose Israel, and whose continued support of the people of His choice came to depend more and more on ethical conditions.

It was natural, therefore, that Israel's religion, originating in a historical event, came to have historical form, though the ascription of later legislation to Moses obscures the full operation of this tendency. Myth, cult and custom are all given historical form.[2] God is known by what He does for Israel, and history is charged with the fullest meaning that can be ascribed to it. Particular events become sacramental, charged with the whole doctrine of God, just as the sacraments of baptism and the Lord's Supper are charged by St. Paul with his whole doctrine of Christ. The wealth of Israel's religious ideas depends on the amplitude of this realm of revelation. We have only to contrast it with that of revelation in Islam to see the difference between wealth and poverty explained. As has been said of Muhammad,[3] 'Belief . . . in himself was the dogma which he taught himself first, and afterwards taught others.' He wrought no miracles; these were replaced by the one miracle of the Kur'an, which is throughout dominated by the consciousness of a single man.

---

[1] Cf. W. J. Phythian-Adams, *The Call of Israel*, pp. 180ff.
[2] Weiser, *Glaube und Geschichte im Alten Testament*, pp. 19ff.
[3] D. S. Margoliouth, *Mohammed*, p. 79.

However genuine his faith, his interpretation of the past and present became more and more subordinate to his own interests as the prophet of Allah. In Muhammad, we have the psychical factor in history at its maximum. Israel also has its own great prophetic figures, from Moses onwards, but they are none of them of this ego-centric type; they subordinate themselves not only to God but to the history in which God acts, and they base their faith on that history, reinterpreted according to the needs of their successive times. Thus, both the objective and the subjective factors receive recognition. The revelation was dynamic and fluid, not static and stereotyped—until Judaism stereotyped it into the religion of a book, and then like Islam had to meet its subsequent needs with the theory of an unwritten Law.

The psychical factor of faith also transforms those events which seemed most contradictory of divine activity on behalf of Israel. The Babylonian Exile seemed to deny God; yet we find two great contemporary prophets transforming that apparent denial into a positive affirmation. Jeremiah consistently interpreted it as necessary and salutary retribution; Deutero-Isaiah lifted it to a new level in his conception of the Suffering Servant. That much-discussed figure seems best explained as that of Israel itself under the category of corporate personality, which allows a continual contraction or expansion in its application. The Servant can be the consciousness of the prophet himself and alone, or he can be the whole people, faithful or unfaithful. In that category of corporate personality, so remote from modern individualism, yet so near to ancient ways of thinking, we have the best explanation of the variety of interpretation amongst modern exegetes. But whatever our conclusion about the historical origin of the Servant, this at least is beyond dispute—that the prophet takes the event of human suffering, undeserved and unexplained, and transforms it into the supreme example of vicarious service and sacrificial offering. This transformation of the event by the faith is of the greatest importance for

Christian theology. Rightly conceived, it supplies a line of approach to the New Testament doctrine of atonement through the sufferings of Christ, which makes it independent of the transactional theories of penalty or satisfaction. The event, as interpreted by faith, is seen to be the actual victory of God over sin and sorrow and death, the three shadows cast by time on eternity.

Perhaps the survival of Israel through six great empires of the ancient world into our modern civilization is the most surprising testimony of all to the significance of the psychical factor in history. Quite apart from any judgment we may pass on the religion itself, here is the outstanding proof that faith can control events by giving them ever new meanings, and so creating new facts. The story of the Jews through the Christian centuries deserves to be better known by us than it is, not only as a rebuke to our pride and to our conscience, but also to show that if history makes men, men make history. Israel, deprived of land and temple, of all that once seemed essential to her faith, showed the power of her faith in a way that recalls Plato's famous test of the justice of the just man crucified. There is a Yiddish tale of starving children in a Jewish attic, whose cry for bread is suddenly stilled when their penniless father declares that this day is a fast unto the Lord. Thus has Israel's spiritual consciousness transformed the material factors of her strange history.

2. THE VALUE OF THE TIME-SERIES

A second line of inquiry is opened by asking what value Israel attached to human life, considered in itself. History is concerned with values rather than with the chronicling of mere events. One of the cardinal questions of a philosophy of history, opening into the greatest issue of metaphysics, concerns the real value of the whole time-series. Can Israel's way of living and attitude to life suggest an answer to this question?

Sir George Adam Smith, in characterizing 'The Hebrew

Genius in the Old Testament',[1] remarks that 'The sheer vitality of the breed, both physical and spiritual, has been so intense and, despite demoralizations and disasters sufficient to have shattered other peoples, has been so enduring, as to imply sources of blood and brain uncommonly rich and vigorous.' We cannot trace back these racial sources with any confidence, beyond a general reference to the nomadic life. But it is easy on most pages of the Old Testament to find evidence of the intensity of Israel's *élan vital*. The passion to live was the more intense because there is no outlook on any real life beyond death till we come to the closing centuries of Israel's development—'in Sheol who shall give Thee thanks?' The only life an Israelite had, or could have, was lived on this earth, and he evaluated it with a correspondingly intense realism. 'Vanity of vanities' is not Hebraic at all. Naturally it is in the Psalms and the Wisdom literature that we get the clearest descriptions of life. 'What man is he that delights in life, that loves many days to see good fortune?' (Ps. 34:12). Of Wisdom it is said (Prov. 3:16), 'Length of days is in her right hand, and in her left hand wealth and honour.' The wisdom of the venerable Eliphaz can paint no more attractive picture of the reward of the good man than this (Job 5:24-6):

'Thou shalt know that thy tent is in peace;
And thou shalt visit thy habitation and shalt miss nothing.
Thou shalt know also that thy seed shall be great,
And thine offspring as the herbage of the earth.
Thou shalt come to thy grave in firm strength
As a shock of corn cometh up in its season.'

The aged Barzillai had lost the savour of life at eighty, and had, therefore, nothing more for which to look than to be buried in the ancestral grave (2 Sam. 19:35 f.) and to commend his son to David's patronage.

Israel's conception of human personality allowed no room for asceticism, for the self was the animated body, with a

[1] *The Legacy of Israel* (ed. by E. R. Bevan and C. Singer), p. 2.

quasi-consciousness diffused through all its members. Just
as the only hope of life after death had to come, when it did
come, in the form of a doctrine of resurrection of the body,
so the present life consisted in the fullest use of all the physical
capacities. That Hebrew word which is rendered 'peace'
(*shalom*) means much more often 'welfare', the completeness
of health and prosperity in the unfettered exercise of every
normal function.

It is quite true that the Hebrew range of experience is in
some directions narrowly limited. The fact that the religious
lyric is its only artistic product reminds us of its aesthetic
shortcomings, whilst its intellectual life showed no native
development into philosophic or scientific inquiry, as with the
Greeks, but was harnessed to the practical affairs of life.
This very concentration, however, may have been necessary
to create the ethical productivity of Israel. 'Above all
guarding watch thine heart, for from *it* are the outgoings of
life' (Prov. 4:23). Here, as so often elsewhere in the Old
Testament, the heart stands for the volitional and not the
emotional centre. It is the will that is primary in Hebrew
psychology, and that is significant for the characteristic of
Hebrew life which most concerns us here, viz., its sense of
actuality, the fact that life is engaged in producing something
new, positive, of real worth to man and God.

This sense of actuality is most illustrated in the peculiar
phenomena of prophetic symbolism, by which is meant, not
the mere use of figures of speech, but the actual doing of
deeds in connection with the prophetic word, such as the
breaking of an earthenware flask by Jeremiah to represent
the breaking of Judah and Jerusalem (19:1 ff.).[1] This was not
simply a dramatic act, an oriental gesture accompanying the
public utterance; it was done privately, prior to the utterance, in the presence of chosen witnesses, and had formal

[1] See my essay on 'Prophetic Symbolism' in *Old Testament Essays*,
published by Griffin, for the Society of Old Testament Study, 1927.
Whatever the formal affinity of such acts with those of primitive magic,
they gain a new quality and meaning in Hebrew prophecy, as does the
psychology of 'ecstasy' itself.

affinity with the ritual breaking of earthenware in connection
with curses, found at a lower level of culture, as a form of
symbolic magic. It shows the significance of the deed—the
spoken word, with its intrinsic power, is itself a deed. An
Arab whose son was cursed by an enemy threw the boy
down, that the curse might fly over him.[1] We see the same
sense of the actuality of the deed in the interpretation of
actual experiences of life, such as Hosea's marriage. The
symbolic deed or experience is conceived as itself a part of the
ultimate reality of things which the prophet declares; it is
like the Pauline conception of the Christian's present experience of the Holy Spirit as an ἀρραβών of what is to come,
that is, not a mere symbol, but a portion given in advance
of the whole. Nothing could express more strongly than this
prophetic symbolism the sense of the actuality of human life
and its worth to God. Human actions may fall into the
appointed scheme of God's purpose, but they add something
to that purpose—a quality of depth, of existence in a new
category, to use our modern terminology. Jeremiah was a
thought of God before he existed (Duhm)—'Before I formed
thee I knew thee'; but Jeremiah's life added a new quality of
actuality to that thought, as does the artistic creation to the
artistic vision.

All this way of conceiving human life matches Israel's
conception of the divine. God is the living God, that is the
active God, known by what He does, to whom can be
ascribed a heart, that is a will, comparable with man's
(Jer. 3:15, etc.). With Him is the fountain of life (Ps. 36:9),
and He is the God of the life-spirits of all flesh (Num. 27:16).
He is working out something actual on the arena of earth,
not contemplating a foregone conclusion. Israel knew nothing
of the Greek contrast of time and eternity: the reality of God
was even conceived within a sort of super-human temporality,
which closely linked the temporal and the eternal.

It may be urged in criticism of any discussion of the
achievement of actual values in the time-series, whether by

[1] J. Wellhausen, *Reste arabischen Heidentums*, p. 139 n. 4.

Israel or by any other nation, that we are arguing in a circle. Our standard of values is itself derived from the history to which we apply it. This is true and inevitable. We can never gain a standpoint, much less a standard, outside the world of history of which we are ourselves a part. The problem of norms was not solved by Troeltsch, the most distinguished of modern thinkers along this line of inquiry. But is not this yet another form of that duality within unity which belongs to all our consciousness? We meet it in the psychological inseparability of the subject–object relation, and in the metaphysical blending of the human and divine in religious experience. On any theory of authority, the only ultimate court of appeal must be God, and if God is active in human history, the evidence of His presence must be in that activity itself, and from it, and so from Him, our ultimate standard of values must always be derived. Why then should Israel not create in her divinely-controlled history standards by which all history has to be judged?

3. The Unity of History

In the third place, Israel has a very definite contribution to make towards the conception of the unity of all human history. From the side of philosophy, it has long been recognized that we owe to Christianity the first conception of a history of the world. We shall not find it in the greatest historian of Greece, Thucydides, in spite of his acute penetration into the political factors of the struggle between Athens and Sparta. As for the Greek philosophers, as Rickert remarks, 'Whilst the gaze of the Greek thinkers either rests on the perpetual rhythm of events, or is turned to the picture of a realm of supernatural, but unhistorical and timeless forms, Christianity saw the essential nature of the world in the relation of its historical process to God.'[1] All peoples of the earth were bound to seek after God, the Creator of the world, and all men were derived from a single pair. It was

[1] *Die Philosophie im xx Jahrhundert*, edited by W. Windelband, Vol. II, p. 121.

Christianity which taught men to say with the poet Francis
Thompson, 'I view all mundane happenings with the Fall for
one terminus and the Millennium for the other.'[1] But, true
as this is (of the period before modern science had profoundly
modified this simple view of the world-order), we must not
forget that Christianity itself borrowed this very conception
from Israel. Augustine's *City of God* could not have been
written without the Old Testament. It might more truth-
fully be claimed, with R. H. Charles, that 'Daniel was the
first to teach the unity of all human history, and that every
fresh phase of this history was a further stage in the development of God's purposes'.[2] Dr. Charles argues that, whilst
the great prophets dealt with the destinies of this nation or
of that, they took no comprehensive view of the history of
the world as a whole. Yet it is to them that the Book of
Daniel itself ultimately owes its comprehensive vision of a
divine purpose, extending beyond the borders of Israel, and
subduing the other nations to that purpose. It was Isaiah
who said of Sennacherib's invasion, 'Ye looked not unto Him
that had done this' (22:11), and as Duhm remarks, to say
that God makes history is religiously a much more important
and valuable saying than that God has made the world.
Alone amongst the nations of the ancient East, Israel 'pos-
sesses a conception of history, in the sense of finding a deeper
meaning in the course of events'.[3] The historical records of
Egypt, Babylon and Assyria do not point forward with such
a faith to such a goal. The Magian cycles of Persia are no
more than a mythological parallel to the Danielic idea of the
secular kingdoms, even though they may have helped to
shape that idea. It is significant that the only approach elsewhere to the idea of a final goal of all human history should
be due, as it is in Ancient Persia, to the prophetic reform of a
traditional religion. We may be very conscious to-day how
much more complex is the problem than Israel conceived it

---

[1] *The Life of Francis Thompson*, by Everard Meynell, p. 313.
[2] *Commentary on Daniel*, p. cxiv.
[3] Jirku, *Geschichte des Volkes Israel*, p. 12.

to be, but it is to the religious instinct of Israel that the conception of the unity of history is due.

One important difference between Israel's conception of this unity and that which prevails to-day should be noted carefully, and this is in regard to the idea of 'progress'. It is natural for us, under the spell of evolution, to conceive Israel's history as a gradual development, as in some respects it certainly is. We may be tempted to apply to that history the dictum of Troeltsch, 'The absolute *in* the relative, yet not fully and finally in it, but always pressing towards fresh forms of self-expression and so effecting the mutual criticism of its relative individualizations—such is the last word of the philosophy of history.'[1] But, whatever truth there may be in the principle as a modern approach to the problem, it is certainly not true of the essential characteristics of Israel's own consciousness. Evolution is there replaced by the whole group of ideas which we loosely bring together as 'eschatology'. There is no seed of inevitable progress, and no guarantee of it in the nature of things. Israel's hope is in God, and the new Jerusalem necessarily comes from above, though it is built on earth. The unity of history is found not in man but in the purpose of God, who will ultimately establish His kingdom *ab extra*. Moreover, this eschatology is not an 'other-worldly' dualism which condemns and rejects the life of time, but a sublimation of its best, with an elimination of its worst—a very different thing. If the eschatological conception seems to us both inconsistent with the facts of history, and an anthropomorphic abandonment of genuine philosophic thought about the universe, we can still ask whether it does not preserve an essential element in a right view of the universe, and whether there is not a beneficent ministry of illusion in all our thinking, theological or philosophical. If the unity of human history is to be found in God—and where else can we hope to find it?—it is not necessarily irrational to conceive that that history will have

[1] In his article, 'Historiography', *Encyclopaedia of Religion and Ethics*, Vol. VI, p. 722.

an end, as it had a beginning, even though its eternal significance passes beyond all the temporal features of a beginning
and an end. It might well prove that the truest way of
conceiving the eternal is itself in terms of the purpose of
God, as for example, Professor Pringle Pattison has suggested.[1] If so, then Israel has surely given us our most
emphatic demonstration of eternity in terms of time and of
the ultimate unity of history in the purpose of God.

4. THE RELATION OF TRANSCENDENCE AND IMMANENCE

The fourth and last point is the attitude of Israel to the
relation of the transcendent and immanent. Here again we
must carefully distinguish the categories that suit *us* and
those which were native to Israel. From our modern standpoint, Israel's thought of God was strongly anthropomorphic
throughout. But in fact Israel drew a sharp distinction
between the essential nature of God and of man which is often
overlooked. It is seen most clearly in Isaiah's reference
(31:3) to Egypt:

> Now the Egyptians are men and not God,
> And their horses flesh and not spirit.

When we interpret that in the light of the unity of the
animal world with man, and of Hebrew parallelism, we see
that it indicates the essential distinction of man from God.
Man is 'flesh' (*basar*); God is spirit (*ruach*). There we have,
as Duhm says, with his usual penetration into Hebrew ways
of thinking, the underlying factors of the long struggle of
human history as the Bible conceives it, the key to the whole
subsequent history of religion to 1 Cor. 15. It is in terms of
the relation of flesh and spirit that we must conceive the
relation of the human and the divine, always remembering
that, for Hebrew thought, the flesh is animate and 'psychical'
and includes all the elements of human personality, so long

---

[1] *The Idea of God*, p. 358: 'The eternal view of a time-process is not
the view of all its stages simultaneously, but the view of them as elements or members of a completed purpose.'

as it is animated by the breath-soul. It is only in the post-exilic literature that we see the Ruach of God becoming a permanent element of human personality, instead of an occasional and startling visitor. How important that inner relation of man and God became for St. Paul, and for his πνεῦμα doctrine, is clear to every student of the New Testament. The special gift to prophets and kings and Messianic princes became unconsciously democratized in the psychology of Israel long before the New Testament, and there is no essential dualism in St. Paul's view of the 'flesh'.

But the conception of the activities of the Spirit of God is not the only or, indeed, the chief aspect of our present question. We have to think of the whole relation of the human and divine wills, which is so constantly illustrated in the pages of the Old Testament and remains as much a prob-lem for St. Paul. All we can say here is summed up by that Jewish Rabbi who witnessed and himself accelerated the final tragedy of Israel's corporate life in the Bar-Kochba Revolt, viz., Akiba: 'Everything is foreseen and freewill is given. And the world is judged by grace; and everything is according to work.' Even the Council of Chalcedon could not leave us with more sharply presented antitheses. Yet they are certainly true of Israel's conception of life, however difficult or impossible it may be to reconcile them. There is, however, one line of Israel's experience that does point towards a solution. That line runs through the prophetic consciousness. Here we have at once the sharpest antithesis to idolatry (at least in the later representatives of prophecy), and the conviction that the unseen imageless God can yet enter into the human conscience and clothe Himself with it, so that it cannot be alien to Him. Surely the emphasis on imageless religion, the complement to that on the prophetic consciousness, is the deepest Old Testament preparation for the Christian doctrine of the Incarnation—with its essential principle that personality alone, not its material semblance, is capable of becoming the temple of God on earth, the visible union of the human and the divine, the transcendent and the immanent, the eternal and the temporal. That God should trust men to recognize the divine, within and through the human, is the supreme proof of man's spiritual capacity.[1]

The four lines of thought here suggested, rather than developed, viz., the psychical factor of faith, the pragmatism of moral values, the unity of history in the purpose of God, and the fundamental and ultimate fellowship of the human and divine, may be viewed as an attempt to reconstruct the old and discredited 'argument from prophecy' in a new way. To find merely verbal or factual resemblances between the records of Israel's history and the origins of the Christian faith proves nothing. Revelation does not depend on the ingenuities of a cross-word puzzle. But when we get beneath the surface of the record to the actual course of the history, as we have tried to do in this book, when we face the facts and evaluate the factors of that history, we may be able to trace an impressive *spiritual* continuity, and a resistless moral energy, which both call for explanation in themselves and point forward to something beyond themselves. The history of Israel is itself so great a fact, and the appearance of a control over the working of its human agents is so impressive a factor, that we can hardly escape the challenge— is not the greatest and most comprehensive fact of that history that it reveals God, and is He not Himself the ultimate and supreme factor, hidden within the religious experience which created the history and issued in the Christ?

[1] Cf. A L. Lilley, *Religion and Revelation*, p. 110.

APPENDIX

I. SELECT BIBLIOGRAPHY

Baynes, N. H. *Israel amongst the Nations*. 1927 (chiefly for the full bibliography).

Bertholet, A. *Kulturgeschichte Israels*. 1920 (Eng. trans. by A. K. Dallas, *A History of Hebrew Civilization*, 1926).

Bevan, E. *Jerusalem under the High-Priests*. 1924.

Bright, J. *A History of Israel*. 1960.

Browne, L. E. *Early Judaism*. 1920.

Bury, J. B., Cook, S. A., Adcock, F. E., and Charlesworth, M. P. *CAH = The Cambridge Ancient History*. 1923–34. Vols. I–X.

Causse, A. *Les Dispersés d'Israël*. 1929.

Cooke, G. A. *A Text-book of North-Semitic Inscriptions*. 1903.

Cowley, A. *Aramaic Papyri of the Fifth Century*. 1923.

Dennefeld, L. *Histoire d'Israël et de l'ancien Orient*. 1935.

Desnoyers, L. *Histoire du Peuple Hébreu des Juges à la Captivité*.

   I. La période des Juges   1922
   II. Saül et David   1930
   III. Salomon   1930

Dhorme, E. *La Religion des Hébreux nomades*, 1937 (for history of patriarchal age).

Gressmann, H. *ATAT² = Altorientalische Texte zum alten Testament*, ed. 2. 1926.

 ABAT² = Altorientalische Bilder zum alten Testament, ed. 2. 1927.

Grollenberg, L. H. *Atlas of the Bible*, Eng. trans. by J. M. H. Reid and H. H. Rowley. 1956.

Guthe, H. *Geschichte des Volkes Israel*, ed. 3. 1914.

Hall, H. R. *The Ancient History of the Near East*, ed. 8. 1932.

Jirku, A. *Geschichte des Volkes Israel*. 1931.

Jones, A. H. M. *The Herods of Judaea*. 1938.

Juster, J. *Les Juifs dans l'Empire Romain*. 1914.

Kent, C. F. and Riggs, J. S. *History of the Hebrew and Jewish People*.

      I. From the Settlement in Canaan to the Division of the Kingdom. 1923.

      II. From the Division of the Kingdom to the Fall of Jerusalem. 1923.

      III. Babylonian, Persian and Greek Periods. 1899.

      IV. Maccabean and Roman Periods. 1900.

Kittel, R. *Geschichte des Volkes Israel*.

    I. (ed. 5). 1923   II. (ed. 5). 1922

    III. 1.   1927   III. 2.   1929

Lods, A. *Israël des Origines au milieu du VIII Siècle*. 1930. (Eng. trans. by S. H. Hooke, *Israel from its Beginnings to the Middle of the Eighth Century*. 1932.)

Lods, A. *Les Prophètes d'Israël et les débuts du Judaïsme*. 1935. (Eng. trans. by S. H. Hooke, *The Prophets and the Rise of Judaism*. 1937.)

Meek, T. J. *Hebrew Origins*, 2nd ed. 1950.

Meyer, E. *Die Israeliten und ihre Nachbarstämme*. 1906.

Meyer, E. *Ursprung und Anfänge des Christentums*. II. Die Entwicklung des Judentums und Jesus von Nazaret. 1925.

Noth, M. *Das System der zwölf Stämme Israels*, 1930.

Noth, M. *Die Welt des Alten Testaments*, 3rd ed. 1957.

Noth, M. *The History of Israel*, 2nd Eng. ed. 1960.

Oesterley, W. O. E. and Robinson, T. H. *A History of Israel* (2 Vols.). 1932.

Pritchard, J. B. *A.N.E.T.* = *Ancient Near Eastern Texts, relating to the Old Testament*, 2nd ed. 1955.

Pritchard, J. B. *A.N.E.P.* = *The Ancient Near East in Pictures*, 1954.

Robinson, T. H., Hunkin, J. W., and Burkitt, F. C. *Palestine in General History* (Schweich Lectures). 1929.

Rogers, R. W. *Cuneiform Parallels to the Old Testament*. 1912.

Rowley, H. H. *From Joseph to Joshua*. 1950.

Schlatter, A. *Geschichte Israels von Alexander dem Grossen bis Hadrian*, ed. 3. 1925.

Schürer, E. *Geschichte des jüdischen Volkes im Zeitalter Jesu Christi*, ed. 4.
  I. 1909   II. 1907   III. 1909
(Eng. trans. *A History of the Jewish People in the Time of Jesus Christ*. Div. I, Vols. 1 and 2 by J. Macpherson. 1890. Div. II, Vols. 1–3, by S. Taylor and P. Christie, 1893–94.)

Sellin, E. *Geschichte des israelitisch-jüdischen Volkes*.
  I. 1924   II. 1932

Smith, G. A. *Historical Geography of the Holy Land*, ed. 25. 1931.

Historical Atlas of the Holy Land, ed. 2. 1936.

Stade, B. *Geschichte des Volkes Israel*.
  I. 1886   II. 1888

Wellhausen, J. *Israelitische und Jüdische Geschichte*, ed. 7. 1914.

Wellhausen, J. *Prolegomena zur Geschichte Israels*, ed. 6. 1905. (Eng. trans. by J. S. Black and A. Menzies, *Prolegomena to the History of Israel*, 1885.)

Wellhausen, J. *Sketch of the History of Israel and Judah*, ed. 3 (from *Ency. Brit.*). 1891.

Wright, G. E. *Biblical Archaeology*, 2nd ed. 1962.

Wright, G. E. *An Introduction to Biblical Archaeology*. 1960.

Wright, G. E. and Filson, F. V. *Westminster Historical Atlas to the Bible*. Revised ed. 1956.

II. THE TRIBES OF ISRAEL

The genealogical scheme of Gen. 29: 31 ff.

JACOB

LEAH	RACHEL
Reuben[1]	
Simeon[2]	
Levi[3]	
Judah[4]	

BILHAH
Dan[5]
Naphtali[6]

ZILPAH
Gad[7]
Asher[8]

Issachar[9]
Zebulun[10]
(Dinah)[11]

Joseph[12]
Benjamin[13]

References to the chief data are given on the following page. For details of exegesis, reference should be made to the Commentary on Genesis (International Critical) by J. Skinner, that on Deuteronomy (ib.) by S. R. Driver, and that on Judges by C. F. Burney. For a general review of the history of these tribal groups, see E. L. Curtis, 'The Tribes of Israel', in *Biblical and Semitic Studies* (Yale University, 1901), and the summary notice in Ch. I, § 4 of the present book.

The three ancient tribal songs are those of Judges 5 (c. 1100 B.C.), Gen. 49 (c. 900 B.C.) and Dt. 33 (c. 800 B.C.); separate elements in each may be older than the songs as a whole.

[1] Judges 5:15, 16 (non-participant); Gen. 49:3, 4, cf. 35:22; Deut. 33:6 (diminished).

[2] Omitted in Jud. 5; Gen. 49:5–7, cf. 34:25ff.; omitted in Dt. 33 (absorbed in Judah?).

[3] Omitted in Jud. 5; Gen. 49:5–7 (secular), cf. 34:25ff.; Dt. 33:8–11 (sacred *class*).

[4] Omitted in Jud. 5; Gen. 49:8–12; Dt. 33:7 (divided from Israel). For its larger Canaanite elements, see Gen. 38.

[5] Jud. 5:17 ('in ships'); Gen. 49:16, 17, cf. Jud. 18; Dt. 33:22.

[6] Jud. 5:18; Gen. 49:21; Dt. 33:23.

[7] Jud. v:17 (Gilead = Gad); Gen. 49:19; Dt. 33:20–21 (cf. Num. 32).

[8] Jud. v:17; Gen. 49:20; Dt. 33:24, 25. There were 'Asaru' in Phoenicia towards end of fourteenth century.

[9] Jud. 5:15; Gen. 49:14, 15 (in servitude to Canaanites); Dt. 33:18, 19.

[10] Jud. 5:18; Gen. 49:13 ('at the haven of the sea'); Dt. 33:18, 19.

[11] Gen. 34; 'Dinah' seems to represent an early clan overcome and absorbed by the Canaanites of Shechem.

[12] Jud. 5:14, where Ephraim and Machir (the chief clan of Manasseh, Num, 26:29) represent 'Joseph'; Gen. 49:22–24; Dt. 33:13–17.

[13] Cf. Gen. 35:18; Jud. 5:14; Gen. 49:27; Dt. 33:12.

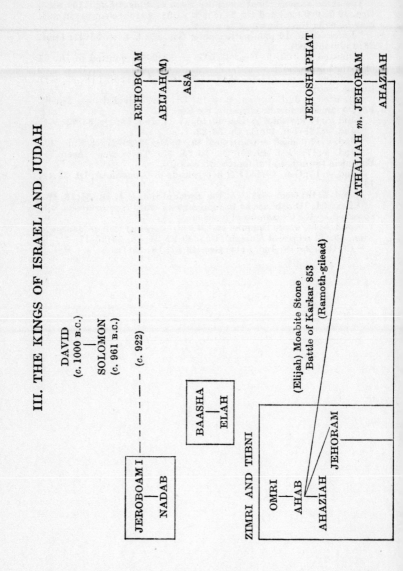

III. THE KINGS OF ISRAEL AND JUDAH

DAVID
(c. 1000 B.C.)

SOLOMON
(c. 961 B.C.)

— — — — — — (c. 922) — — — — — —

REHOBOAM

ABIJAH(M)

ASA

JEHOSHAPHAT

ATHALIAH m. JEHORAM

AHAZIAH

JEROBOAM I

NADAB

BAASHA

ELAH

ZIMRI AND TIBNI

OMRI

AHAB

AHAZIAH

JEHORAM

(Elijah) Moabite Stone
Battle of Karkar 853
(Ramoth-gilead)

Tribute to Assyria, 841

N

JEHU
JEHOAHAZ
JEHOASH
JEROBOAM II
ZECHARIAH

(Amos)
(Hosea)

SHALLUM
Tribute to Assyria, 738
PEKAH
Tribute to Assyria, 734
Galilee depopulated, 733
Damascus captured, 732

MENAHEM
PEKAHIAH

HOSHEA
Fall of Samaria, 722 B.C.

JEHOASH
AMAZIAH
AZARIAH (UZZIAH)

(Isaiah)

JOTHAM
AHAZ

HEZEKIAH
MANASSEH
AMON
JOSIAH
JEHOAHAZ (Shallum)

Book of Deuteronomy, 621
(Megiddo, 608)
JEHOIAKIM
JEHOIACHIN
Battle of Carchemish, 605
ZEDEKIAH
Fall of Jerusalem, 536 B.C.

IV. THE IMPERIAL BACKGROUNDS

(with some important dates)

EGYPT	PALESTINE	MESOPOTAMIA
	3000– Babylonian control and in-	Hammurabi about 1790–
	c. 1600 fluence	1750
Expulsion of the Hyksos, 1580	1483 Battle of Megiddo, establishing Egyptian power	
Thutmosis III 1483–1450		
Amenophis III 1412–1370		
Amenophis IV (Ikhnaton) 1370–1354	c. 1400 Tell el-Amarna Letters (*Habiru* invasions)	(Hittite Empire, 13th cent.)
Rameses II 1301–1233		
Merneptah 1233–1223	c. 1200 Approximate date of settlement of 'Josephite' Hebrews and of Philistines	
Sheshonk 950–929		(*Assyria*)
	853 Karkar (not in O.T.)	Shalmaneser III 859–825
	841 Jehu pays tribute (not in O.T.)	

Egypt	Palestine	Mesopotamia
		Tiglath-Pileser III (= Pul) 745–727
	738 Menahem pays tribute (to Pul, 2 Kings 15:19, 20)	
	734 Syro-Ephraimitic War (Is. 7)	Sargon 722–705
	728 Ahaz pays tribute (2 Kings 16:8)	Sennacherib 704–682
	722 Fall of Samaria (2 Kings 18)	612 Fall of Nineveh
Pharaoh Neco 609–593		(*Neo-Babylonians*)
	608 Megiddo	Nebuchadrezzar (604–562)
	605 Battle of Carchemish	
	597 First Deportation	
	586 Second Deportation	(*Persia*) Cyrus (538–529)
	538 'Return' begins	Cambyses (529–522)
	521–516 Building of Second Temple	Darius (521–485)
		Xerxes I (485–464)
Elephantine Papyri (fifth century)	444–432 Governorship of Nehemiah	Artaxerxes I (464–425)
		Xerxes II (424)
		Darius II (424–405)
	397 Return of Ezra	Artaxerxes II (404–358)
	353 Deportation of Jews?	Artaxerxes III (Ochus) (358–338)
(*Greece*)	334–323 Alexander the Great	Darius III (338–331)

EGYPT	PALESTINE	MESOPOTAMIA
(Ptolemies) (305–30 B.C.)		Seleucids Antiochus the Great (223–187)
	312–198 Ptolemaic control	
	198–143 Seleucid control	Antiochus Epiphanes (175–163)
	168 Desecration of Temple	
	167 Maccabean Revolt	Demetrius I (162–150)
	165 Reconsecration of Temple (Judas)	Alex. Balas (150–145)
	143–142 Independence recognized (Simon)	
	134–65 Hasmonaean rulers	
(Rome)	63 Pompey's intervention	
	37–4 B.C. Herod the Great	
	A.D. 66–70 Jewish War and Fall of Jerusalem	

INDEX OF SUBJECTS

INDEX OF SCRIPTURE REFERENCES